THE SILVER LINK LIBRARY OF RAILWAY MODELLING

●

THE NEWCOMER'S GUIDE TO MODEL RAILWAYS

'Deltic' No D9017 runs light under clear signals on the author's layout.

THE SILVER LINK LIBRARY OF
RAILWAY MODELLING
•
THE NEWCOMER'S
GUIDE TO
MODEL RAILWAYS

A STEP-BY-STEP GUIDE TO THE
COMPLETE MODEL RAILWAY

Brian Lambert

Silver Link Publishing Ltd

Dedicated to SML

First published in 2009

British Library Cataloguing in Publication Data

A catalogue record for this book is available from the British Library.

ISBN 978 1 85794 329 0

Silver Link Publishing Ltd
The Trundle
Ringstead Road
Great Addington
Kettering
Northants NN14 4BW

Tel/Fax: 01536 330588
email: sales@nostalgiacollection.com
Website: www.nostalgiacollection.com

Printed and bound in the Czech Republic

All drawings and pictures are by the author unless otherwise credited.
www.brian-lambert.co.uk

A Silver Link book
from
The NOSTALGIA *Collection*

ACKNOWLEDGEMENTS

I would like to thank the following for their assistance, or their products being referenced, in the preparation of this book: Antex (Electronics) Ltd; Bachmann Europe Ltd; Dapol Model Railways; Digitrax Inc; Expo Drills and Tools; Express Models; Gaugemaster Controls Plc; Hornby Hobbies Ltd; Javis Scenic Materials; Lenz Elektronik GmbH; Maplin Electronics; Marklin Inc; Metcalfe Models & Toys Ltd; Moseley Railway Trust; Peco Group of Companies; Scalescenes; Slaters Plastikard Ltd; South West Digital Ltd; Squires Tools Ltd; Superquick Models; TCS (Train Control Systems); Trix Railways; Vincent Bailey, artist.

In addition I am indebted to The Model Shop, Woodchurch, Nr Ashford, Kent TN26 3QE (+44(0)1233-860008) who supplied many items for the photographs in this book.

Finally, my daughter Sarah Lambert for taking many of the pictures.

CONTENTS

PREFACE

I have been involved in model railways for far too many years now and though my interests are mainly in the UK 'OO' gauge scale, this book is written to help all modellers, no matter what the chosen gauge.

For me, it all began way back in the 1950s when, as a small child, I was given a Tri-ang Railways 'Princess Elizabeth' train set for Christmas. It was nothing more than a simple oval of clip-together plastic 'Standard' track, a tender loco and two carriages with a battery-powered controller. Christmas Day saw me as the onlooker! My father and my uncle were kept very busy erecting the train set on the front room floor, then they spent the afternoon thoroughly checking to see that it worked correctly. I actually never got to run the set on that day!

In later years, but still as a pre-teenager, I was able to have a 'train set' layout permanently set up in my bedroom. As the years passed, by now into my early teens, I was able to build a medium-sized layout in an unused box room, which lasted for a number of years. Finally the call of youthful adulthood, together with its many attractions, beckoned and was taking more and more of my free time. So the layout was taken apart and most sold off to a neighbour.

During the earlier years of married life I had the occasional thought of a model railway, and the odd model railway magazine would be obtained and reviewed. A son and daughter were born, and a few years later my son had a simple train set for a present, but this was not a model

railway and slowly the need to build a fully working model railway became more than a desire. After a couple of false starts it was at the beginning of the 1990s that real railway modelling once again took a firm hold on me and eventually a fully working layout emerged.

Since those teenage years, having moved home several times and had a couple of model railway false starts, I decided it was time to knuckle down and seriously start to build a decent model. So 'Ridgley Vale' was drawn up and became my first attempt at a portable exhibition-quality layout. Later I tried building another portable exhibition layout, but for whatever reason it never really got beyond the track-laying stage! A further house move then saw me inherit half of a double garage, so I just had to have another layout, and 'Elmswood & Elmswood Central' was created, only this time it was a fixed layout that was destined never to leave home.

My wife Sue at times helps to build the odd bit of scenery, which she delights in pointing out to any layout visitors as being 'hers'! However, without her encouragement I wouldn't be where I am today.

The following pages will, I believe, help and guide the beginner into the hobby and, of course, also be of help to anyone who has already started to build a model railway. Readers will, page by page, gain more information and learn the basics to allow them to build and operate a model railway rather than just run a train set.

Class 37 No 37698 *Coedbach* emerges from the tunnel's darkness on the author's layout.

1
A DECISION ON SIZE

Model railways, as the name implies, are based on small-scale representations of the real thing, so the choice for new modellers is the actual model's scale, which is usually determined by the availability of space for what you wish to represent, and the skill level you possess – whether as a new modeller you want to open a box and run a train immediately, known as 'ready to run' (RTR), or build most items yourself from a mixture of kits or totally self-build, known a 'scratch building'. Perhaps the best skill of all to have is patience! A model railway takes time to build, but the time spent in building it is very rewarding and satisfying.

Most people will come to model railways through being either being given as a present or buying for themselves a train set. Sometimes the returning modeller will find an old set from many years ago, hidden away in the back of a cupboard or in a loft, and decide to 'have a play',

then the model railway bug starts to bite and with time he or she will become a more serious modeller.

Expanding the train set beyond what is 'in the box', which is normally a basic oval of track, one or two locos, a few carriages or trucks and a basic controller, often follows fairly quickly from the initial box opening! Quite often newcomers will remain working in the scale of that first train set, as this is what they already have and are used to. Some, however, will opt to go for a larger or even a smaller scale, once they have examined the various scales available and decided what will fit into the space available for the layout.

So what is scale and track gauge?

Scale is the relationship of the model to the real thing. The real thing could be described as being

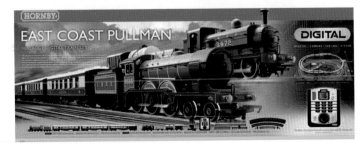

Two typical train sets: the upper one is a conventional dc set ('analogue') while the lower set is a digital or DCC control set. *Courtesy of and © copyright Hornby Hobbies Ltd*

'1 to 1' (1:1) scale, so an exact half-size model would be at a scale of 1:2, where as 1 is the real size and 2 is the model in half size. Therefore a quarter-size model would be at 1:4, while a model which is 1/100th of the full size is at 1:100 scale.

Because most of the world has gone metric there is another range of scale terminology that is often used in model railways: the reference, for example, to 4mm/ft (4 millimetres to 1 imperial foot) or 2mm/ft (2 millimetres to 1 imperial foot) are but two examples. Thus a UK 'OO' modeller may be quoted as working in 4mm/ft, 1:76th scale, 16.5mm (more of this later) or just plain 'OO'!

Track gauge is as confusing as scale, but I'll try and explain. Track gauge is the distance between the inner faces of the two running rails. In the UK and many parts of the rest of the world railways use a gauge of 4ft 8½in, or 1435mm. In railway modelling there are, depending on scale, many track gauges. For example, 'N' gauge (1:148 scale in the UK) has a track gauge of 9mm. UK 'OO' has a gauge of 16.5mm between the rails, while '1' gauge has a massive 45mm between the running rails. Even more confusion can exist when 'fine scale' models are considered.

Three scales of the same type of Class 66 locomotive: the largest is in 'G' scale, centre is 'OO' and the smallest 'N' scale. *Courtesy of British Railway Modelling magazine*

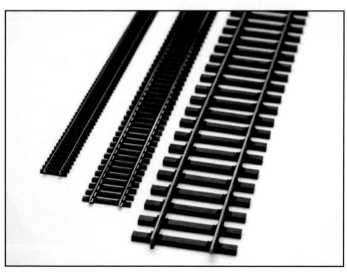

Three gauges of track: from left to right they are is 'N', 'OO'/'HO' and 'O'. The distance or 'gauge' between the inner faces of the rails of each track is 9mm ('N'), 16.5mm ('OO'/'HO') and 32mm ('O').

Standard gauges: small to large

'T' gauge has earned the right to claim to be the smallest commercially made ready-to-run electrically powered railway system. Sold currently only in continental outline it is an incredibly small size and is produced to a scale of 1:450 or 0.002 inches to the foot, and has a track gauge of 3mm.

'ZZ' gauge is the next largest scale (if 'largest' is the correct term!). Again sold in continental outline models, it has a scale size of 1:300 running on 4.8mm-gauge track.

'Z' gauge was probably the smallest working model railway available until the arrival of 'ZZ' and latterly 'T' gauges. Sold in continental outline, it is 1:220 scale and has a track gauge of 6.5mm. I have seen a complete layout built and running in the space occupied by a removed cathode ray tube in an old 14-inch TV cabinet.

'N' gauge is next, with a scale of 1:160, but UK modellers will recognise this as being 1:148; the track is at 9mm gauge. This is the first scale we meet where more than one size of scale exists on the same gauge of track! This scale is at times referred to as 2mm scale, which is not quite correct. Track and rolling stock are available as kit-built and ready-to-run.

'2mm' or 'OOO' scale runs on a track of 9.5mm gauge and is to 1:152.1 scale. This is mainly a British scale from the 1930s when 'OO' was halved. In this scale most modellers scratch-build their locos and rolling stock.

'TT' or 3mm gauge came to the UK from America, the initials standing for 'Table Top'. It has a track gauge of 12mm and in the UK is to a scale of 3mm/ft or 1:101 (USA 2.54mm/ft or 1:120). Tri-ang Railways took up the cause in the UK and for a short while produced ready-to-run models, but they ceased production and British outline models are now only currently available as kits.

'HO' gauge is the truer scale for 16.5mm track. It has a scale of 3.5mm/ft or 1:87, and is used internationally apart from in Britain. 'HO' stock will happily run on 'OO' track as they both share the same track gauge. Several attempts have been made to try and get the UK to drop 'OO' in favour of the truer 'HO' scale, but they have so far always been stopped, as 'OO' has far too big a hold on the UK market. Items for this scale are available as ready-to-run or can be scratch-built or built from kits.

'OO' gauge is the UK's answer to 16.5mm scale. The track is at 16.5mm (same as 'HO') and has a scale of 4mm/ft or 1:76. The over-sized rolling stock on the 16.5mm track is due to the fact that the early UK manufactures couldn't obtain electric motors small enough to fit inside a true-scale (3.5mm or 'HO') loco body, so 'OO' was born at an over-scale size running on near-scale track. Again, all items for this scale are available as ready-to-run or can be scratch-built or made up from kits. Live-steam electrically controlled locos are now available in 'OO'.

'EM' gauge is the first attempt by British modellers to obtain as near true 4mm scale running as possible. While still not an exact 4mm scale, it is still at 1:76 or 4mm/ft, but the track gauge is widened out to 18.2mm. Many modellers in this scale will opt to replace the standard 'OO' wheel sets of production models with their own EM gauge wheels. There are also, of course, kit-built locos and rolling stock available.

'P4' and 'S4' gauges are the second, mainly UK, attempts at the true 4mm scale, often called 'fine scale'. 'S4' stands for 'Scalefour', while 'P4' is 'Protofour'. The track gauge is at 18.83mm and again it is to a 4mm/ft or 1:76 scale, although purists of this gauge will say it is actually at a 1:76.2 scale, which is the true 4mm scale. Track is normally hand-built; some straight track is available ready-made, but all pointwork is hand-built, as are most of the locos and rolling stock, though some modellers will convert a good-quality 'OO' loco body by grafting it onto a hand-built chassis.

'S' gauge is the only truly imperial gauge left, and is not often seen nowadays, as all items have to

A scene from the author's former 'OO' 4mm/ft layout 'Ridgley Vale'.

be hand-built. It has a track gauge of ⅞ inch or 22.22mm, and has a scale size of ³⁄₁₆ inch to the foot, or 1:64.

'O' gauge has its roots at the beginning of mass-produced model railways. It has a track gauge of 32mm and is 7mm/ft or 1:43 scale in the UK (1:48 in the USA). Much credit has to be given to the early manufactures of this scale in the UK – Bassett-Lowke and Hornby – who sold thousands of clockwork and electric tinplate train sets. There is a small supply of ready-to-run items available, but mainly modellers in this scale build their own stock from kits or scratch-build. Track is both commercially available and sold as individual items to allow modellers to build their own track and pointwork. In this gauge live steam operation is a viable option running alongside electrically powered locos.

'1' gauge is perhaps the grandfather of all the gauges, for it was the Edwardian modeller who first started this large-scale model railway. It was very popular until the First World War, when it began to lose much of its sales; however, it was resurrected later, in the 1960s. It has a track gauge of 45mm and is to a scale of 9.5mm/ft at 1:32 scale, or the slightly larger but equally compatible size of 10mm/foot, or 1:30. Here again – perhaps even more so – live steam is an

option. Outdoors is where this gauge really scores, though of course most other gauges can be used outside too. Perhaps this is not a gauge to be taken up by a beginner, but it is certainly a gauge and scale to be seriously considered by those who like model engineering and who would like to produce a model without any compromises in scale or detail. (See also 'G' scale in the 'Narrow gauge' section below.)

Then of course there are the much larger gauges, such as 2.5in (Gauge 3), 3.5in, 5in and 7.5in, often running live-steam locos with their drivers sitting behind on specially constructed wagons. Other gauges include 7in, 12.25in and 15in, but all these are outside of the scope of this book.

So, in the standard gauges there are plenty of choices. Your overall space, budget and perhaps even your eyesight and dexterity will play a factor in which gauge is your final choice. Mainly most will opt to operate in 'N', 'OO'/'HO' or 'O'.

Other factors, such as the representation of the location of the model – British or continental – will have a smaller, but still important, effect on your decision, as too will the physical location of the model: 'N' gauge outdoors isn't viable, but indoors will offer far more track per square metre than 'OO' or any of the larger scales.

Narrow gauge

Narrow gauge is defined as any track width below standard gauge (4ft 8½in), and includes 3ft 6in and metre gauge, but for model railway purposes I'll keep to those narrow gauges that are more at home in the home!

'OO9' and 'HOe' have the same 9mm track with a scale of 4mm/ft and 1:76 for 'OO9' or 3.5mm/ft at 1:87 for 'HOe'. UK outline stock is limited to mainly kit-built items, while continental ranges are available as both ready-to-run and kits.

'HOn3' has a track gauge of 10.5mm to a scale of 3.5mm/ft at 1:87. It is mainly a USA-sized system used to depict that country's 3-foot-gauge railways. Some items are available as ready-to-run, but most are in kit form.

'HOm' runs on 12mm gauge track and is to the 'HO' scale of 3.5mm/ft or 1:87. It is very popular with Swiss modellers at it represents the metre-gauge railways of that country in the popular 'HO' size. Many items are available as ready-to-run.

'OOn3' is not often found, but is to a scale of 4mm/ft on a track gauge of 12mm, and is often used to model the Irish metre-gauge railways. Normally items are only available as kits to self-build.

'O-16.5' is 16.5mm gauge ('OO'/'HO') at 7mm/ft or 1:42.5 scale. This scale uses 'OO' or 'HO' chassis with kit-built bodies. No ready-to-run models are known of.

'SM 32' has a 32mm ('O') track gauge with a scale of 16mm/ft. Most models are kit-built but there is a good supply of this gauge in the UK with some RTR items available from specialist retailers.

'G' gauge has a track gauge of 45mm ('1' gauge) and is commonly known as 1:22.5 scale, although other manufacturers produce products that range from 1:20.3 to 1:32. Many will know this scale as being represented more popularly by LGB; it was introduced by Lehmann under the brand name 'LGB' ('Lehmann Gross Bahnor', or 'Lehmann Big Train'), but was more recently available from numerous suppliers including Marklin, following the bankruptcy of the Lehmann company. It is ideal for the garden and can, of course, also be used indoors. More recent models have ventured into replicas of full-size UK railway locos. 'G' gauge is readily available from many UK retailers.

These are the most common gauges; there are several others, but these tend to be of minority interest and cannot realistically be covered by this book.

A narrow gauge Ashover Light Railway Baldwin locomotive. *Drawing reproduced by kind permission of the artist, Vincent Bailey; Moseley Railway Trust (www.mrt.org.uk)*

2
A HOME FOR THE RAILWAY

Where is the best place for your model railway? Anywhere really, so long as it is dry and free from excessive dust or can be covered over if there is any danger of dust being spread over it. Never run a train set (sorry, model railway!) directly on a carpeted floor – all you will succeed in doing is introducing fluff and dust into the loco's gearing and electrical pick-ups, resulting in a failed loco shortly afterwards! Build your layout on a firm baseboard and ideally try and keep the board at least a metre (39 inches) above the floor. Some will advocate even higher baseboard heights, but I've found that anything over 1 metre high isn't practicable for the younger viewer, and even some of the older constructors will struggle to gain access to the rear of a layout once it exceeds that height.

Where to put your layout is entirely up to you: be it loft; garage, shed, spare room, bedroom, basement, or even the lounge, it matters not, so long as you build with the approval and consent of your partner, parent, etc. I have seen small layouts in lounges – but never construct something that will look totally out of place or cause domestic disharmony (you have been warned!).

Pros and cons

Loft
The loft is ideal for being out of the way, and can offer a large area for use. Extremes of temperature are a problem, but that can be helped by a window or extractor fan being used in the summer. If you can afford it, air-conditioning or a climate control unit will ensure a constant temperature and humidity level, but these units are expensive both to purchase and run. Lack of height to walk around, especially in some

modern buildings, can be a problem, and don't forget that water storage tanks may take up a lot of space. Never, ever, cut or alter any trusses or other roof timbers unless you really like having your roof in your lounge! Also, consider the thickness (depth) of rafters or joists, which will need to be sheeted over to allow a flat and safe walking area. This area must support the weight of at least two adults, and be covered by at least 18-20mm boarding or floorboards. Watch out for cables and pipes that run on top of, or close to the top of, joists when securing the flooring – also allow suitable access points for future building repairs and maintenance, etc. Don't forget that you will probably need both lighting and power supplies installed, as often there is no mains power in a loft! If in doubt, consult a professional architect and electrician.

Garage
Much the same can be said as for lofts, due to the extremes of temperature – though probably not quite so hot in the summer! Dust and insects (spiders especially) will be a problem here. Sealing up the main access door will help with the dust problem, assuming there is alternative access and the main garage door is not required. Usually you will find only one course of brick or blockwork between the inside and external of a garage – ie there is no cavity – though this shouldn't interfere too much with the modelling process! But be aware that there may only be approximately 4½ inches of brickwork between you and your neighbour's garage internal wall if your garages are attached, so caution is needed when drilling holes for fixings, etc. Electricity in garages is normally not a problem as often both power and lighting are provided; even if not, it is not often a serious issue to get power into a

An 'N' scale model railway under construction in a specially converted loft space. This is a portable layout and can be easily taken apart section by section, passed down through the loft hatch and assembled elsewhere, such as at exhibitions or a friend's home. Quite often loft layouts are more permanent and built around the walls or the framing of the loft area.

garage. A nice level concrete floor will normally be found, but treat with caution, as concrete floors are renowned for producing excessive dust and making your feet feel uncomfortable. Consider a carpet or other floor covering for the main areas. Some form of heating will be needed for winter use.

Shed

These are similar to garages, but are often located remotely from the main house. Normally of wooden construction, they provide little or no thermal insulation at all, so consider installing a suitable insulation material and internal cladding to the walls, ceilings and even the floor. Almost certainly there won't be any electrical supplies, so the cost of installing the supply, sockets and lighting will need to be included in the overall budget, which may become excessive. Shed size is another governing factor: if you can only accommodate an 8ft x 6ft shed and you plan to work in 'OO' gauge or larger you may find space is rather tight! Sheds should really be built on a solid base – patio slabs or

similar are ideal, as these will ensure that over time the shed won't slowly sink into the ground due to all the weight being placed upon the flooring and walls. Insect invasion will almost certainly be the norm, so always de-spider/de-ant and remove all the cobwebs before a running session.

Spare room

This is probably one of the best locations for human comfort! Electricity will already be installed and often central heating too. There are no major issues with insect invasion and it will often be carpeted. I would recommend a carpet protector, however. Perhaps some sort of PVC sheet or a nice clean plastic tarpaulin covering the best Axminster will ensure there are no accidental spills suddenly appearing as marks or stains on the carpet – note that there is no known remedy for removing spilled superglue from carpet tufts! Care should be exercised if you're securing the baseboards to the room's walls; check for buried cables and pipes in the walls before drilling by using a buried service

This garden shed has been fully insulated and has had all the walls, ceiling and floor lined; good overhead lighting and power sockets have also been installed. The 'N' gauge layout is seen here still under construction; while it is an option that is not always taken, the layout is portable and not fixed to the shed's inner walls. Note the use of the 'helix' loops nearest the camera, which allow a train to ascend or descend from one level to another in a relatively small area and without the need of long ramp sections such as that seen on the extreme right.

locator device to scan the wall beforehand. As with a shed, the available space may restrict your ideas, so always plan your layout well before commencing any construction. It is far easier to alter a paper or PC drawing than change the timber baseboards installed in a room.

Lounge or other room

Your layout here will probably be restricted in size and will often only be an end-to-end layout that can be incorporated in the room together with all its other furniture. The actual construction should be in harmony with the room: use a better quality of timber to face the viewable edges of the baseboard and perhaps, if possible, even consider having a hinged L-shaped cover to fully enclose the layout when it is not in use. This cover would also keep any dust off the layout. Remember, this is possibly the main living area, so be extra careful when using liquids such as glues, solvents and paints on the model; don't allow anything to be spilled and damage the surroundings – repairs will be costly and domestic disharmony guaranteed!

Cellar or basement

These can be used and are often ideal for the model railway as they are not normally a fully habitable room. In the UK their use is probably restricted, as cellars are normally only found in older properties, and one major drawback is damp because they are normally below ground or street level, so this can become a serious problem. Only use this area if the room is damp-proof and of sound construction, then it is a good home for the model railway. If the cellar is damp you will need to employ a specialist damp-proofing company to eradicate the damp ingress, which may well be at considerable expense! Electricity for lighting, heating and providing power for the layout can normally be easily installed from the rooms above; this work should be carried out only by a qualified electrician. Some form of floor covering may be well worth investing in, as often cellar floors are of concrete construction, which will create dust and also become cold for the feet. Consider laying a carpet or other suitable flooring materials such as a laminate floor or even sheet or tile vinyl flooring. Dry-lining the walls may be a further option to enhance the comfort of the cellar for the modeller.

Specially built hobby room

Unless you have unlimited funds, a hobby room specially dedicated to the model railway will be little else more than a pipe dream for most. Such rooms are often a brick-built extension to the main house, and will be built with ample electric lighting, power, heating and cooling for all-year-round use. The use of 'daylight' lighting enhances the model and can perhaps even be dimmed to low levels to allow 'night-time' running with all the buildings on the model internally illuminated.

Out of doors

This offers the modeller a completely new dimension. The relatively large area available and dealing with vegetation that is on a 1:1 scale can be quite daunting. Virtually all gauges from 'OO'/'HO' upwards will run outdoors, but some very special trackbed precautions are required, which is really a topic for a book in its own right and cannot be covered here. Remember, too, that mains-voltage electricity out of doors is extremely dangerous, so always keep the mains voltages safely indoors in the dry!

3
A SOLID BASE

Having found a suitable home for the layout we now need to build a base to support the track and scenery. This is called the baseboard.

There are several methods of constructing a baseboard, and most do not require a degree in carpentry. However, if you cannot be bothered with the effort of full baseboard construction or you just don't have the facilities to cut timber, etc, you can obtain one or more baseboard sections in kit form, available from several commercial suppliers. A quick thumb through any of the monthly railway modelling magazine advertisements will provide a shortlist of suppliers. These kits are supplied either as a set size per baseboard or made to your own size specification. They are normally delivered to you in a flat pack kit and all that is needed is a screwdriver, hammer and some woodworking PVA glue to assemble.

Solid-topped baseboards

For many years these have typically been constructed from 2in x 1in (44mm x 21mm) planed square edged (PSE) timber, placed with its narrow edge up to the baseboard and arranged in a grid pattern of bracing squares of approximately 1 foot (300mm) to around 15 inches (400mm). Larger sizes of timber can be used, but this can add extra weight – see below. I wouldn't recommend using any timber smaller than 44mm x 21mm as warping or twisting on a longer run can result.

Construction is no more complex than cutting each piece of timber to the required size with the aid of a mitre block and hand saw, or a mitre frame hand saw, or perhaps an electric compound saw, often called a 'chop saw'. The two most important things are that the timber is

A mitre frame hand saw being used to cut square a piece of PSE timber for a baseboard.

cut exactly to the correct length and that the ends are cut perfectly square; here the use of the mitre block, mitre hand saw or compound saw is invaluable.

Measure exactly and cut the four outer framing timbers first. These are then fixed together with woodworking PVA glue and fastened with wood screws to make the appropriate rectangle or square shape. To prevent end grain splitting, possibly the best method is to use a suitably sized pilot drill to make a hole right through the outer timber and into the abutting timber's end grain before the woodscrew is inserted.

After the four outer frame pieces are assembled, the top surface sheet is fitted, either glued and pinned, or glued and screwed if the top is solid enough to prevent the screws from pulling through. Now measure and cut all the internal bracing timbers, then drill a hole of 15mm to 20mm diameter into the centre of the broader side of each before fitting them; the top of the hole should be approximately 5-10mm down from the top of the timber. These holes

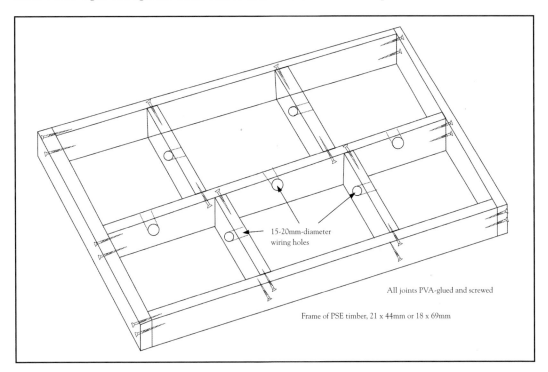

15-20mm-diameter wiring holes

All joints PVA-glued and screwed

Frame of PSE timber, 21 x 44mm or 18 x 69mm

Above Figure 1: Simple baseboard framing. The whole top is subsequently sheeted over and all the track and scenery is built onto this flat surface.

Right A cut-away section of a solid baseboard top reveals the basic timber structure below. Note the simple square-cut butt joints of the framing. All joints have been screwed and glued with PVA woodworking adhesive and the top has also been PVA-glued and pinned in place. Note the 16mm-diameter hole drilled centrally in all the internal cross bracing to allow for later wiring runs.

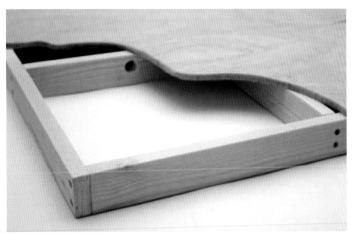

will later allow all the layout's wiring to pass between each bay of the baseboard. The reason for pre-drilling the holes before fitting is that it is much harder to drill them once the timbers are fixed in place! Now fit, by gluing and screwing, the longer cross bearer(s), then fit all the shorter right-angle timber bearers; these will need to be slightly staggered to allow the woodscrews to be inserted from the central longer bearers – see Figure 1. Don't forget to run PVA glue along the top edges of all cross bearers before fitting them as this will help bond the baseboard top to the bearers. You should also pin from the top of the baseboard down into the cross bearers to make the final construction as strong and rigid as possible.

There is no reason other than cost and weight why deeper timber than the 44mm depth can't be used. In fact, the deeper the timber is, the more its thickness can be marginally reduced! Ideally, when using any timber for framing always allow the timber lengths to lay flat and unwrapped for around 48 hours in the room where the layout is to be constructed; this will 'condition' the timber and allow it to expand or contract with the room temperature and humidity. While it may not be actually possible to lay out the timbers in the layout's final location (as with portable layouts), the timber should still be 'conditioned' indoors for at least 48 hours before use.

Where inclines or underpasses are to be modelled, the baseboard surface is cut along the required length and width of the trackbed and the surface gently raised or lowered from the datum of the flat board. Initially, on rising track a thin fillet of wood is let in under the section to be raised with its outer edges resting on the flat baseboard surface. Spaced over a set distance, thicker fillets are added until a smooth transition from flat to gradient is produced. Once the track base is rising correctly, T-shaped risers are used to support the elevated sections in much the same way as with L-girder baseboard construction (see below). A gradient of about 1 in 40 seems to be about the sharpest up which 'OO'/'HO' locos can comfortably pull a reasonable length of coaches or wagons without too much loss of power or slipping.

A simpler method of making a rising or falling gradient, particularly where solid sheeted baseboard tops are used, are the gradient supports produced by several manufactures. For example, in 'OO' Hornby produce an Inclined and high-

Figure 2: Constructing a rising trackbed

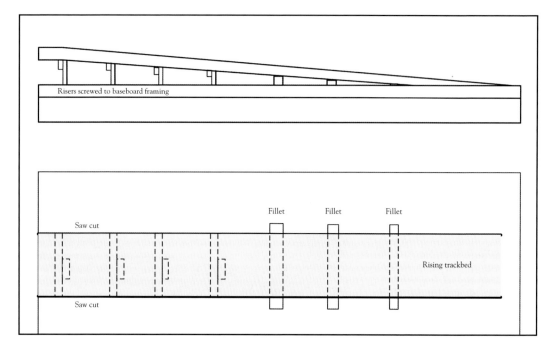

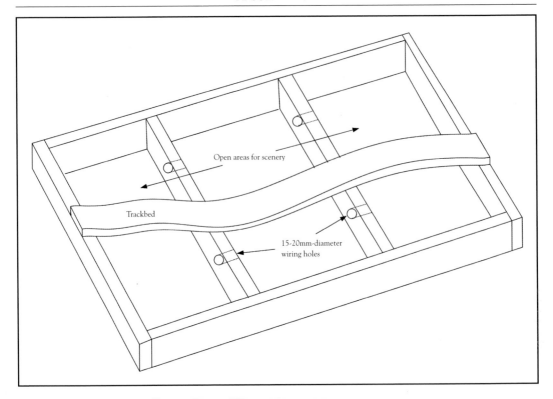

Figure 3: A basic open-frame baseboard

level Pier system, while Noch manufactures a continuous incline and Woodland Scenics produces a flexible foam incline in various incline gradients to suit 'N' and 'OO'/'HO' gauges.

Open-top baseboards

These can be assembled by using a similar method of frame construction, but this style of baseboard allows a more natural-looking scene to be depicted as the scenery can rise or fall above or below the trackbed. A very simple idea is shown in Figure 3. By cutting a notch into the cross bracing timbers, a river or road can then pass under the trackbed, the depth of the notch being determined by the overall depth of the framing timbers; they should never be more than 50% of the depth to avoid causing the timber frame to become excessively weakened.

Plywood box construction

This gives rigidity and lightness to the baseboard and is ideal for the portable layout. Typically, 4mm-6mm ply is made up into a box section

with PSE timber of between 9mm and 12mm thick in between, making an overall thickness of between 17mm and 24mm. The depth of the panel is best kept to around 70-100mm to avoid any possibility of longitudinal sagging. Internal bracing timbers running from top to bottom and giving additional support are added during construction, especially where any T-joints with other cross members occur (see Figure 4). Also these supports will aid the insertion of woodscrews to allow 'pull up' of the joint.

Plywood on its own can be substituted for the PSE timber of the earlier all-wooden frames and can produce a very strong yet reasonably light frame. The minimum thickness to use is 9mm WBP ply, and keep the sections not less than 70mm deep to prevent longitudinal sagging. At all external corners and any internal T-joints there is a need to fit a short piece of timber block or fillet to allow the ply to be firmly fixed at right-angles. These blocks are PVA glued to both faces of the ply and the joint is then secured by suitable woodscrews driven through the ply into the blocks.

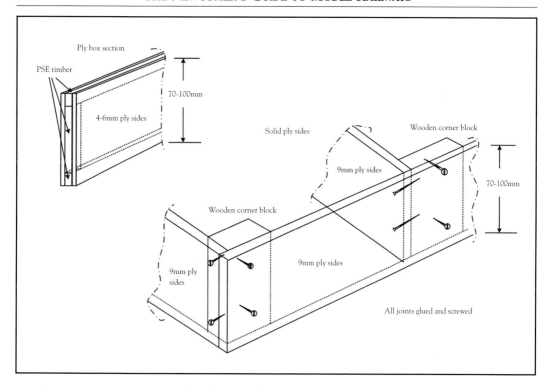

Above **Figure 4: Plywood box construction**

Below **Figure 5: The basics of L-girder construction**

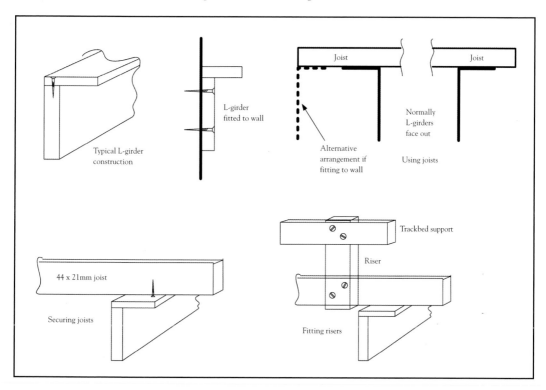

L-girder construction

This is another method of open-top baseboard construction, which is only really suitable for permanent layouts. It is formed from either one solid length of 3in x 2in (69mm x 44mm) timber, or, perhaps easier to obtain, 3in x ¾in (69mm x 18mm) PSE and 2in x ½in (44 x 12mm) PSE timbers screwed and PVA-glued together to make an 'L' shape. If you're lucky and can readily access cheap 3in x 2in timber, this can have a rectangular section of approximately 1in x 2in (25mm x 50mm) cut out to produce an L-shape. This cutting will require some serious woodworking machinery, such as a bench-mounted circular saw, so it is much easier to screw and glue together two lengths of timber to form the basic 'L' shape. This shape is extremely strong in the downward direction and is also very resistant to bowing sideways. It may seem strange that where screwed and glued timber is being used to make the 'L' that the top rail isn't the same thickness as the horizontal rail. This is because I have discovered that ½in x 2in (12mm x 44mm) is adequate and, when the glue has dried, the resulting L-girder is extremely strong – why use a thicker and more expensive timber? 'L' beams can then be held up adjacent to each other by suitable legs spaced at approximately 6-foot intervals, and braced across the lower end at approximately 300mm above floor level to

The basic L-girder shape: the construction is detailed in the text. The timber shown is all PSE with the upright section 69mm x 18mm and the top section 44mm x 12mm, glued with woodworking PVA and screwed together.

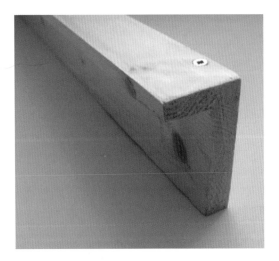

prevent any spreading of the legs. Alternatively one L-section is screwed to the wall and the other outer 'L' supported on legs as above. Two parallel L-girders are the foundation of each span.

Once the two L-girders are in place, they are held parallel to each other with cross joists that can often extend out beyond the L-girders. These are made from 2in x 1in (44mm x 21mm) timbers screwed in place at 12-inch (300mm) intervals. It must be remembered that the joists are fixed without any glue, being just screwed up from underneath through the top 'L' baton.

The trackbed board on open-top layouts is either screwed directly to the tops of the joists for level or flat running, or supported above the joints on risers and cross 'trackbed supports'. The risers are made from more 44mm x 21mm PSE and the trackbed supports are from the same timber set at 90 degrees to the upright risers. These are glued with PVA woodworking glue and screwed together to make the 'T' shape. The riser is then loosely G-clamped to the joist at the correct location and its height adjusted. When all is correct the G-clamp is tightened and two woodscrews are driven through the riser into the joist; the risers aren't glued to the joists. When all is secure the G-clamp is removed.

MDF (Medium Density Fibreboard)

I have experimented with this board and used the 9mm-thick variety, cut to a depth of approximately 100mm, as an overall framing instead of the more usual 44mm x 21mm timber (much like the ply sides discussed previously). It proved to be more than suitable and isn't as heavy to lift as a conventionally framed baseboard. However, I did pre-drill a series of 1½in (35mm) holes into the internal sections with the aid of a hole saw in an electric drill, which reduced its overall weight; the holes also allow ease of wiring. In addition, once the framing was made up, I coated every section of the MDF with a quick-drying varnish to protect the frames from any ingress of moisture. I also braced every corner and T-joint with some PSE timber fillets (21mm x 44mm) cut to fit inside each right-angled joint to give really firm bracing at the corners, again as per the ply construction.

Portable baseboards

These will need to be made according to three major criteria. One is that the completed board is transportable; second, that it can be manhandled with some ease; third, that it needs to be protected during storage and transportation to ensure that all the delicate track and scenery will remain intact.

Where size is concerned I would recommend a maximum size per board no greater than 4ft x 2ft (1200mm x 600mm); much over this size and it becomes a two-person lift, and getting anything larger up or down stairs and through doorways becomes that much more difficult, if not near impossible at times!

Protecting the layout is, of course, vital, and consideration can be given to one of three methods: casing, crating or stacking.

Casing involves taking each board and building a simple light fabrication of perhaps 3mm ply or MDF with some lightweight timber internal bracing to form a box that fits over the whole board and provides total cover. (See Figure 6.)

Crating consists of two identically sized baseboards held scenic side to scenic side by two end plates, and where necessary a light sheeting of ply is added to both long sides to form a totally enclosed box. The other option is to make two identically sized boards that are hinged and can fold up together; the height of the hinge pillars is determined by the height of the scenery on the two boards plus a small amount for clearance. (See Figures 7 and 8.)

Stacking is where two or three baseboards are slid into a simple frame, made in most cases of timber. Once fully in place either a locking baton is bolted across the full height of the stack or alternatively each board is bolted to the framework to prevent it from sliding out of the frame. (See Figures 9 and 10.)

Figure 6: Casing as a protection for a portable layout

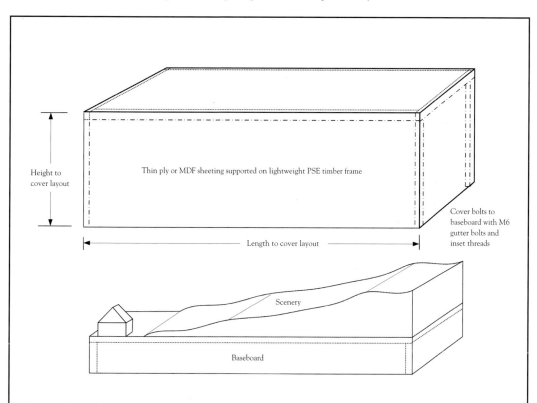

Height to cover layout

Thin ply or MDF sheeting supported on lightweight PSE timber frame

Length to cover layout

Cover bolts to baseboard with M6 gutter bolts and inset threads

Scenery

Baseboard

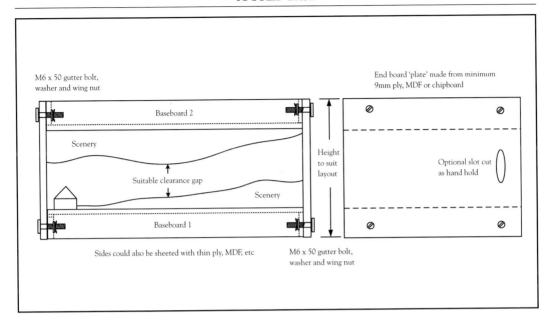

Above Figure 7: Crating two identically sized baseboards one above the other separated by two end plates

Below Figure 8: Two baseboards hinged together, the height of the hinge pillars keeping them separated

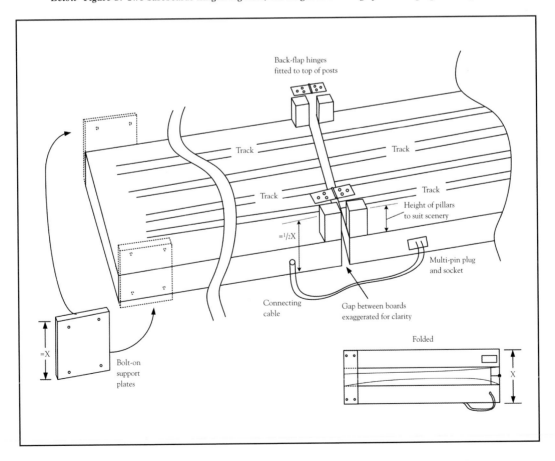

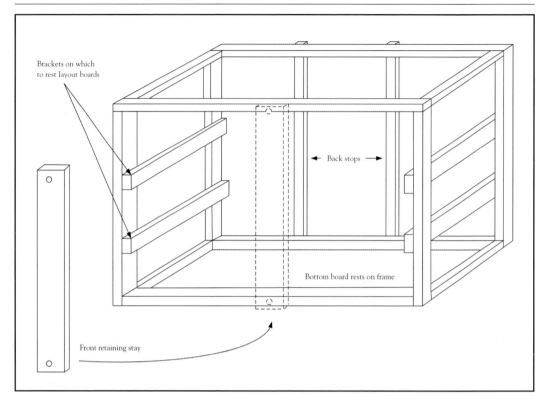

Brackets on which
to rest layout boards

Back stops

Bottom board rests on frame

Front retaining stay

Above Figure 9: A stacking crate

Below Figure 10: The stacking crate shown with the baseboards in place

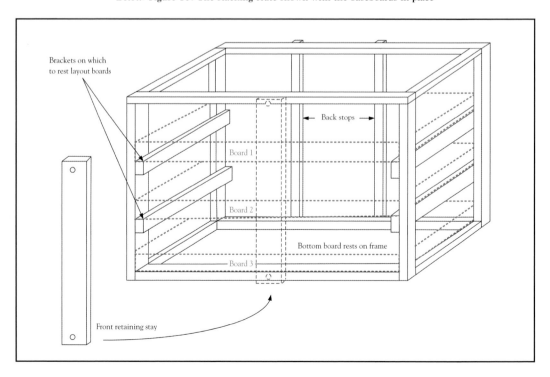

Brackets on which
to rest layout boards

Back stops

Board 1

Board 2

Bottom board rests on frame

Board 3

Front retaining stay

Baseboard surfaces

Plywood

This is a good material to work with. Ply is ideally suited to both 'flat-topped' (fully sheeted) and 'open-top' construction and allows reasonably sized boards to be built without being over heavy. 9mm is the ideal thickness as this will curve gently up or down from the horizontal where any transition ramps are required. 6mm ply can be used, but the main disadvantages of this thickness are noise, as it starts to become a skin like a drum, and it is rather thin to accept any woodscrews for fixing point motors, for example. However, 6mm ply is ideal for any non-tracked areas where lightness of the layout for handling is required, for example town scenes or flat country areas of farmland, etc.

Sundeala

This is extremely easy to push track pins into, and it holds them in place quite well afterwards. Its sound-deadening qualities are good, and it too can be gently flexed up or down to allow for transition slopes. It is often available from good model shops in a pre-cut sheet size of 2ft x 4ft (600mm x 1200mm), with a thickness of ⅜in (9mm), which is convenient for carrying home. Its main disadvantages, if there are any, are that it is quite difficult to cut, and almost impossible to sand an edge smooth. It doesn't hold woodscrews particularly well and is a little too soft to prevent woodscrews pulling through its surface when screwed into the framing. It is therefore far easier to PVA glue and pin Sundeala in place onto the frame. It must also be well supported on timber formed into a grid of approximately 12-inch (300mm) squares or sagging of the board may occur.

MDF

This material needs to be cut very carefully as the dust is harmful. It also suffers from possible moisture ingress unless it is sealed completely, and is really hard to drive pins into. It cuts easily with a normal panel saw, electric jig or circular saw, and can also be sanded smooth (both with suitable safety precautions observed). It will probably slightly increase any sound from moving trains, , but this is often only marginal.

Chipboard

Half-inch (12mm) chipboard is quite good for model railway baseboard tops. It is cheap to buy and is readily available in pre-cut sizes. It accepts woodscrews and is quite a hard surface. Cutting and sanding present no serious problems (with safety precautions observed). The main disadvantage is the considerable weight that it adds to the construction, but this only applies to layouts that have to be moved frequently or are designed to be fully portable.

Softboard

This is sometimes referred to as insulation or pin board, and I would not recommend this material as this fails to hold track pins securely. It is far too soft and will often warp or sag even when supported at 300mm centres!

In short, I would recommend that the builder goes for a top made from plywood, or MDF if preferred.

Some modellers have used flush panel doors, and I have read reports of others using 50mm-thick expanded foam sheet or polystyrene sheet as baseboard tops. While these may work for some, I have serious doubts. Doors are an extremely awkward size and the physical effort required to pick them up and move them is something I personally wouldn't want to face, especially if scenery has been added – they are heavy and cumbersome! I have never seen foam board or thick sheets of polystyrene used, but their propensity to sag over time is a concern. Also remember that any solvent spilled onto a polystyrene sheet will result in a large hole appearing before your eyes! So beware if you are going to use this material, and keep all solvents well away from the layout – liquid poly cement and some rail-cleaning fluids will be the major contenders!

Supports or legs

Here the main issue is whether the layout is to be portable or permanently fixed in place. The height also needs to be considered. This will depend upon your personal preference, but mainly a minimum of 39 inches (1 metre) to baseboard top is recommended. Lower or higher

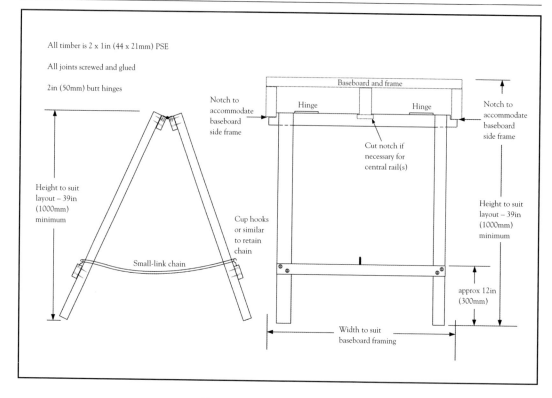

All timber is 2 x 1in (44 x 21mm) PSE

All joints screwed and glued

2in (50mm) butt hinges

Notch to accommodate baseboard side frame

Baseboard and frame

Hinge

Hinge

Notch to accommodate baseboard side frame

Cut notch if necessary for central rail(s)

Height to suit layout – 39in (1000mm) minimum

Cup hooks or similar to retain chain

Small-link chain

Height to suit layout – 39in (1000mm) minimum

approx 12in (300mm)

Width to suit baseboard framing

Figure 11: Trestle layout supports

levels can be used, but where a layout is destined for the exhibition circuit, the height of the viewing public should be considered too: it is not much good having a children's 'Thomas' layout set at 39 inches above floor level, as the viewers are going to be mainly young children who won't be able to see it at that height!

Portable layouts

Portable layouts can have support legs that are self-contained on each individual board and can even be made to fold up within the confines of the board, or they can be a separate self-supporting structure, such as trestles.

Trestles can be simply home-made from 21mm x 44mm PSE, a pair of butt hinges and some means of preventing them from 'performing the splits', such as a small diameter rope or small linked chain between the two supporting legs. Both offer a minor amount of adjustment to the overall layout height, which can be set by opening or closing the legs, especially useful when at an exhibitions, where the floors aren't always level.

Ready-made trestles are available and are often of good solid quality. The only drawback with these is their height, which is restricted to that set by the manufacturer and may subsequently be too low for a model railway.

'Up and under' legs are the second option for portable layouts. They are made from 21mm x 44mm PSE, hinged onto another piece of 21mm x 44mm timber fixed to the underside of the baseboard at the required position when folded up. To enable the hinging and folding movement, use 1¼in (30mm) back flap hinges, to pivot the legs up under the baseboards. Cross braces are fitted between the two uprights some 12 inches (300mm) above floor level, as in the trestle construction, then an angled brace is locked between the leg's cross brace and one of the framing timbers underneath the baseboard at roughly 45 degrees. Again using back flap hinges, their pivot pins are removed and a suitable replacement, such as a nail or split pin, is used instead (see Figure 12). Once the brace is located in place and the pivot pins are inserted, the legs

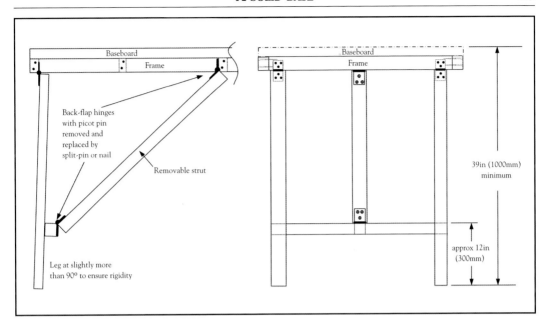

Above Figure 12: 'Up and under' legs

Below Figure 13: Pocketed legs

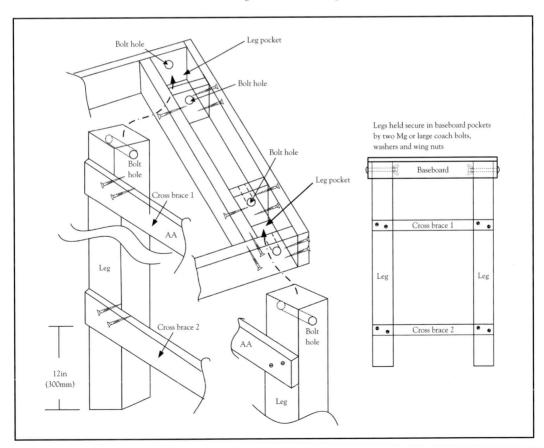

Left An L-girder construction layout being installed in a garage. The fixed supporting leg can be seen in the corner of the front, while the rear 'L' members are turned to face into the centre of the layout and securely fixed to the wall. A flat trackbed of 9mm ply has been partly laid onto the joists and is waiting for the connecting sections to be added before track-laying commences.

Below left This picture shows the 'foundations' of the layout. The two longitudinal 'L' beams can be seen, together with the cross joists held in place by screws driven up through the top portion of the 'L' into the joist. The risers are fitted onto the joists with woodscrews; having been G-clamped in place at the correct track height, the risers are then drilled and screwed to hold them securely in place. Once secured the G-clamp is removed.

Where the L-girder timbers are not long enough to run the full length of the layout, fix a 'joining plate' across the two abutting sections. The plate is made from the same timber as used for the 'L' upright, and is glued and screwed across the jointed timbers. The top section of the 'L' shown here is able to continue without a joint. The track bed is made from 9mm ply, which is also jointed underneath by the 'plating' method where necessary. As this is a DCC layout, the partly hidden black object sitting on top of the left-hand L section is a DCC Automatic Reverse Loop Module.

become very rigid. Note that the leg is actually is just over the 90-degree position when locked down to aid stability.

Pocketed legs are often made from 44mm x 44mm (2in x 2in) PSE timber or other suitably sized timber, and are located into the underside of the baseboard into pre-made compartments or pockets in the corners of the outer framing. They are then held in place with the aid of a through coach bolt, washer and wing nut on the inside. Often these legs are in rigid or bolt-together pairs, held together securely by two smaller-sized timber cross braces (see Figure 13).

Permanent layouts

Permanent layouts will require a stronger and more solid form of support leg, and here the use of fixed legs is the norm. Timber produced mainly for stud wall construction is an ideal medium for permanent layout legs, and is sold as 63mm x 38mm CSL timber. This is pre-sanded and has all four corners semi-rounded. Simply cut square to the required length and fix to the layout framing with woodscrews and some woodworking PVA glue. Additional lower-level cross bracing timbers can be fitted if needed to prevent movement; these need only be made from some 12mm x 32mm PSE and fixed to the legs at around 300mm above floor level.

Fix the baseboard rear timbers to the walls of the room if possible; ensure they are fitted level and use plastic wall plugs and suitably long screws to hold the timber to the wall. Always use an electronic buried services locator tool to carry out a survey of the wall for any possible buried services (electric cables, gas or water pipes, etc) that may be hidden from view deep inside the wall before drilling any holes.

4
THE TRACK

Types of track

Model railway track is available in three basic forms. When manufactured in rigid sections, it is sometimes called 'sectional' or more often referred to as 'Setrack'. Here the track is produced in ready-made lengths of straights, curves and matching pointwork, the curves being pre-set to defined radii; often there are four radii, known as Radius 1 (the tightest curve) to Radius 4, the latter being the largest outside pre-curved sectional track currently available in 'OO'/'HO'. The track is available either as sleepered or with a pre-moulded ballast infill.

Flexible track, with pointwork to suit, allows ready-made lengths of track to be carefully curved to the desired radius and cut to length as required. Its set distance between two adjacent running lines is often closer and therefore a little more prototypical than sectional track.

Hand-built track and pointwork is made to the most exacting standards, and can in the main be considered to be as prototypical as possible in virtually every aspect.

Sectional track is sold by virtually all the major model railway producers and is usually included in train sets. This track system offers beginners an immediate basis on which to build the model railway and get their locos running. Clip-together sections of virtually unbendable track provide a quick way of track-laying, and are joined together to make the simplest oval of track that can be up and running in a few minutes. Later, the addition of a point or two and more track to make another loop, a passing loop or sidings gives extra interest and operating potential. Points can also be used to link concentric loops by what is termed a crossover.

Points on sectional trackwork normally use what is termed an 'insulated frog', which means that no special electrical feeds are needed to power a siding or loop and the points are self-isolating. Thus a loco can be run into a siding or loop and when the points are moved to close the siding the loco can no longer be moved under electrical power until the point is again set for that line. This is a very useful feature and simplifies layout wiring. The disadvantage is the relatively large area of the plastic 'frog', or crossing vee, built into the point; when a loco is passing over the frog, especially when running slowly, it may stall or stutter on the insulated frog section as it loses power.

Most sectional track will space two adjacent lines a little bit further apart than perhaps is considered normal. This extra space between the two tracks helps prevent any two long vehicles, such as long carriages, touching each other when passing on the curves.

Flexible track, as its name suggests, is able to be pre-set to almost any desired curvature. It is usually supplied in 3-foot or sometimes 1-metre lengths with plastic sleepers representing either timber or concrete sleeper types, all factory fitted. Running beneath the rails is a longitudinal sleeper joining web, which is discontinued at every second or third sleeper, alternating from side to side; these gaps in the web allow the length of track to be gently curved or flexed in either direction. The user lays the track by either joining together lengths to make straight runs or by gently pre-curving the track section, then laying it to a predetermined radius and butting it to the last straight section laid. The radius is usually set much larger than that of sectional track: a 24-inch (600mm) radius is usually the tightest for 'OO' or 'HO', and 10 inches (250mm) in 'N' gauge. Of course, in the larger scales the radius is often in feet rather than inches.

Because the rails in each piece of track are the same length, when the length of flexible track is curved, the inner rail will extend beyond the sleeper ends while the outer rail will be shorter than the sleepered area. Thus the rails will need to be cut to length to maintain the correct square rail joint spacing. Cutting the rails will be discussed a little later. Once cut to the correct length, metal rail joiners are slipped onto the ends of one set of rails, and the rails in the next section are then slipped into the open ends of the joiners until the two rail ends abut. The track is then lightly pinned down to the pre-drawn radius.

Pointwork for flexible track is, like sectional track, often sold with either an insulated frog or a live frog. I will be discussing live frogs later on, as these require some special precautions to be taken during track-laying. Normally the two styles of points have identical 'footprints' as far as their area is concerned. The spacing between two adjacent tracks is normally narrower with flexible track, so to overcome any possible collision points on tighter-radius curves, the gaps between the tracks is opened up a little to that of sectional track spacing. However, as most flexible track is laid to around a minimum of 24 inches radius, no problem is normally encountered, unless exceptionally long rolling stock is used. There will often be more configurations of ready-made pointwork available in the flexible track range, such as three-way points, single or double slips, 'Y' points, etc.

Hand-built track is much harder to complete and requires the builder to have good soldering skills and some specialist gauges and jigs available. The sleepers of hand-built track are more often than not made from specially cut pieces of copper-clad material, much like that used on printed circuit boards for electronics, or in the larger scales they are made from real wood. The copper cladding is cut through in the centre of the sleeper to prevent the short circuit that it would cause from rail to rail if not gapped, and

the rails are soldered to the copper at a pre-set distance apart. One rail is normally soldered first throughout its complete length, then, with the aid of a roller gauge or other track gauge, the second rail is slowly soldered to the copper-clad sleepers, checking that the gauge between the two rails is being maintained as the work progresses. Most hand-built rails are sold in 36-inch lengths in either 'bullhead' or 'flat-bottom' profile. Cosmetic rail chairs are added during the soldering process or are added afterwards and held in place with glue. Some track builders will use plastic-sleepered track and fit their rail into the pre-moulded chairs on the sleepers. Others who use wooden sleepers will, depending on scale, use miniature replicas of real rail chairs to hold the rails, while some smaller scales use fine nails driven through the wooden sleeper into the baseboard. The rails are then soldered to the nail heads.

All pointwork is also hand-built and the rail sections are filed down in special jigs to make the live frog crossings and point switch blades. Some points are supplied in kit form with a paper template, which is laid down on a flat surface and the complex pointwork built on top of it.

Model rails tend to be made from three main materials, steel, nickel silver, or brass. Originally the older train sets had track produced from tin plate, which was superseded by steel or brass rails on open spaced metal sleepers. Initially locos were clockwork or live steam, and the type of rail or sleepers didn't really matter that much. The advent of electric locomotives that took their power from the running rails led to the slow demise of metal-sleepered track. Hornby Dublo introduced a three-rail electrically powered train set using a continuous central rail as the power supply and the two running rails as the return. Of course, steel rails suffer from rusting, and gradually manufactures turned away from that material. More modern track is often commercially produced with nickel silver rail, probably the market leader in all track scales and profiles today, as it does not rust and provides an excellent electrical contact path to loco wheels . Brass rail is now quite often the preserve of the larger gauge modeller. Both brass and nickel silver are ideal for the outdoor railway.

Sleepers, on which the rails are supported and separated, are represented in all scales as either wood or concrete examples of the real thing. As yet the real railway's modern all-steel sleeper has still to be modelled (in plastic) by a manufacturer. Copper-clad sleepers are usually a representation of the prototype's wooden sleeper.

Track is commercially available in mainly the two-rail form, but there are some makes still available in the three-rail version. In the early days 'OO'/'HO' trains by Hornby Dublo, Trix, Marklin and some other continental manufactures all used a three-rail or a central-stud system. In the 1950s a company in the UK owned by 'Rovex' sold a two-rail electric train set to Marks & Spencer. Within two years Lines Brothers had acquired the Rovex company and started production under the brand name of Tri-ang Railways, offering a complete two-rail system. They quickly became a market leader alongside Hornby Dublo in the UK's 'OO' scale.

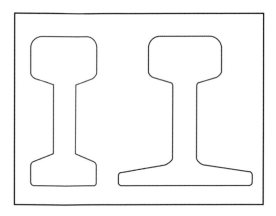

Above Figure 14: bullhead (left) and flat-bottom rail profiles

Below Both styles of rail joiner: that on the nearer rail is the nylon or insulated rail joiner, while furthest is the all-metal rail joiner. These are often referred to as fishplates.

As the 1950s ended Hornby Dublo, which up to that time only produced three-rail systems, had to move to two-rail operation as well. Thus today two-rail model railways are perhaps a more realistic representation of the real thing.

As mentioned previously, rail is produced in two profiles: 'bullhead' and 'flat bottom', and the two styles are shown in end profile in Figure 14. Note that bullhead rail is no longer used on UK main-line railways and can only now be found in some older sidings and on preserved railways; on the model it would only be used to represent pre-1960s main lines.

On full-size railways the rails sit in specially made cast metal chairs and are, depending on type, held secure in the chair with a metal spring clip or a pair of clips known as keys. Bullhead rail is held firmly into the chair by either a hardwood block or a sprung metal key knocked in on the outside of the rail. The rail chair sits on and is secured to the sleeper. Sleepers are normally the full width of the single track plus some additional overhang at each end; they are made from hardwood, concrete or steel, and are supported and held in place normally by stone ballast.

In model form, rail is quoted as being to a 'Code' – for example 'Code 100' or 'Code 55'. The number refers to the actual height of the rail in thousands of an inch ('thou' or 0.001in). Therefore Code 100 rail has a rail profile that is 100 thou (0.100in) high from the underside of the rail foot to the top. Code 100 is often used in 'OO'/'HO' UK layouts, while Code 80 is more often used in 'N' scale. There are other versions of rail available to the fine-scale modeller, such as Code 75 for 'OO'/'HO' and Code 83 for US modellers. Code 55 is the 'N' gauge fine-scale version. Often the same scale of track, but in differing Code sizes, can be connected together with special stepped rail joiners; thus, for example, Code 100 could be connected to Code 75 track. The only problem is that older rolling stock with deeper flanges may ride up on the shallower fine-scale rail as the deeper wheel flanges can touch the rail fixings. This is not such a problem with modern rolling stock (to be safe, assume anything produced since 2002), as these have lower-profile wheels.

Lengths of model railway track are joined together by rail joiners, sometimes referred to as 'fishplates', which is the real railway term for the metal plates that are used to join two abutting lengths of rail. Rail joiners are manufactured to the profile of the foot of the rail in a sort of 'U' shape. They are available in metal or nylon and slide onto the ends of the rails with around half their length on each piece of abutting rail. On the model their purpose is twofold: to hold together the two abutting rails and provide a level and smooth transition between the rails, and usually, though not always, to provide an electrical path from one rail to the other. Nylon rail joiners provide the same alignment as the metal versions, but are used to stop electrical track power flowing from one rail to the next. The nylon joiner often has a small ridge fitted in the centre, to stop one rail end touching the other; if this was to occur, it would negate the desired effect of preventing power flowing from rail to rail. The nylon joiner is more normally referred to as an insulated rail joiner, or IRJ.

Cutting rails

Very occasionally sectional track will need to be cut, while with both flexible and hand-built track it will always be necessary. You can cut the rails with a junior hacksaw, a fine-toothed razor saw, an electrically powered mini drill fitted with an arbour and metal slitting disc, or with one of the commercially available special rail-cutting tools, such as those produced by Xuron.

The easiest to use on smaller gauge track is the Xuron rail cutter, which cuts the rails much like a pair of wire cutters. It may be necessary to use a needle file to smooth off any small burrs remaining on the cut ends of the rail. When using a Xuron cutter always cut rails top to bottom, never side to side.

Electrically powered mini drills, such as those produced by Dremel and Minicraft, make light work of rail cutting and produce a clean burr-free cut. However, the use of eye protection, such as safety goggles or safety glasses, is essential, and keep any onlookers well away from the cutting area, as the slitting disc can easily shatter while turning at high speed and small particles could fly off and injure the operator or bystander.

Using a razor saw is a little slower but can be especially useful if a 'one off' cut is needed.

The use of a rail holding block to prevent the rails being ripped out of their plastic chairs or their soldered locations on copper-clad sleepers is essential when using a razor or hacksaw. The block need be nothing more elaborate than a piece of square-cut PSE timber that is wide enough to span both rails and around 2 to 3 inches in length. It should have two length-wise slots cut into one face at the same distance apart as the two running rails. The block is then placed over the two rails, which locate into the two slots, and is held firmly in place. The square cut end of the block is then used as a guide for the razor saw or hacksaw (see Figure 15). Junior hacksaws on small

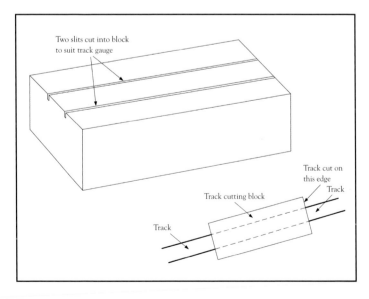

Figure 15: Using a rail-cutting block

gauge track can only be used with the track unlaid; perhaps the easiest way to cut the track is to hold it on the edge of a suitable cutting area away from the baseboard and gently cut through. The use of the cutting block previously mentioned is helpful here too. Hacksaws really are not the ideal tool for small gauge rail cutting, but are of use on the larger gauges of track. Both razor saw and hacksaw cuts will always need a small smooth file to take off any remaining burrs.

Laying flexible track

If the track needs to be curved, this can be carried out with the aid of a pencil line showing the radius required. The line is drawn onto the baseboard with the aid of a pin, a pencil and a length of string, and represents the exact centre line of the track where it will be fitted. The method of doing this is shown in Figure 16. The same method of marking out can be used to make a curved

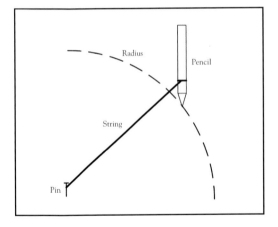

template or a series of differently sized templates, which can be cut from hardboard or 3mm MDF. The templates can then be used against either the inner or outer rails of the proposed curve.

An alternative method of curving track is to use pre-shaped metal or plastic gauges. These are placed between the two rails and the track is then lightly pinned down through the pre-cut slots in the gauge, to retain the curve of the gauge once it is removed. Once each length of track is pinned the gauge is repositioned further around the curve and that track pinned down. The last couple of inches of the gauge should be left in the previously curved and pinned area to ensure that a constant curve is maintained. Tracksetta gauges are a popular make and are available in several scales and in various radii, and even straights.

When curving flexible track I recommend that the length of track be initially pre-curved to just a little more than the required curvature, as it will try to slightly straighten itself again. Carefully pull out the rails from one end by approximately 3 inches (75mm) and gently curve these rails between thumb and finger to just more than the curve required. Refit the rails into the rail chairs in the sleepers, then do the same at the other end, if this is also on a curve. The idea is to try and attain a continuous curve

Left **Figure 16: Drawing out a radius**

Below These four Tracksetta gauges are in two scales and two radii in each gauge. From top to bottom they are 'OO'/'HO' 36-inch, 'OO'/'HO' 24-inch, 'N' 15-inch and finally 'N' 12-inch.

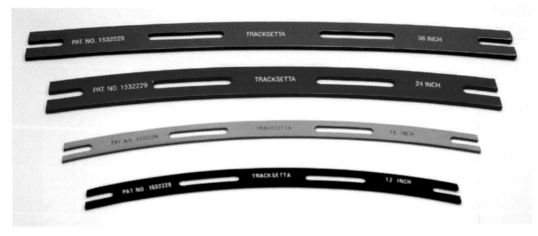

Trimming the outside ends of sleepers to allow converging tracks to fit correctly. Note the two insulated rail joiners (IRJs) fitted to the ends of the two frog rails, as this point is a live frog ('Electrofrog') type.

Trimmed sleeper ends

and prevent the track from straightening up where the rail joiners are fitted, as this could lead to later possible derailments.

When laying long straight lengths of flexible track, I have found the use of a 24-inch (600mm) steel rule invaluable in maintaining a dead straight along the track. The edge of the rule is placed tight up against the outer edge of the rail and the track then pinned down to this alignment. Move the rule along a little at a time, pinning as you go. A line can also be drawn centrally all the way along the length before track laying commences, to further aid true, straight and correct track-to-track parallel alignment. Special between-track distance gauges are available to further aid this process.

Where points are used with flexible track, there is often the need to trim off the outside ends of two or three sleepers from one of the abutting tracks at the vee or frog end of the point, to allow the sleepers to mate into the point's formation correctly. This trimming process is shown in the accompanying photograph. Then two metal rail joiners are slid onto the rail ends of the points, and two infill sleepers are placed under the rail joints.

Joining flexible track is carried out by removing one sleeper from each end of the two lengths of track to be joined together. With the aid of a sharp craft knife, cut up from underneath through the sleeper joining web, and place the

removed sleepers on one side for later reuse. If preferred, and without removing the sleepers, carefully remove the moulded rail chairs from the end sleeper with a sharp craft knife blade by cutting them off under the rails – keep your fingers well away from the cutting area. Slide a rail joiner onto one end of each rail until it is around half way onto the rail. Then carefully offer up the abutting pre-curved or straight track length. Once the two rails are fully inserted into the open ends of the rail joiners, and have been checked by eye that they are correctly fitted onto the bottoms of the rails, pull the rails back a little by approximately 0.5 to 1mm to leave a very small gap between the two abutting rail ends. The idea here is to allow a small expansion gap, which will be required for the summer months' warmer temperatures. Of course, if you are laying track in the middle of a heatwave, there is no need to allow any expansion gaps!

Use a curved gauge, or check by eye against the pre-drawn pencil line, that all is correct. Then pin down the track, ensuring, if it is on a curve, that the radius of the curve is being maintained throughout the join. Once the entire track section has been laid, carefully trim off both of the moulded rail chairs on the formerly removed sleeper, slide the sleeper under the track and position it so that it matches the remainder of the sleepers; add a further trimmed sleeper if necessary to fill any further gaps.

Laying flexible track stage by stage

Top Stage 1: Where a curve is required, draw the centre line of the track onto the baseboard using a pin, string and pencil. The length of string between the pin and pencil is equal to the radius of the curved track.

Middle and bottom Stage 2: The last one or two sleepers are removed by cutting through the soft plastic webbing on the underside of the track. The removed sleepers are retained.

Opposite page

Top Stage 3: The track is curved to the required radius. Here a 24-inch Tracksetta gauge is used to ensure that the correct radius is followed. Note that the inner rail has extended beyond the outer rail. Having removed one sleeper previously, a second will now need to be removed.

Middle Stage 4: The longer rail is cut to the same position as the outer rail. A Xuron rail cutter is being used to trim off the unwanted rail end.

Bottom Stage 5: Rail joiners (fish-plates) are slid onto the rail ends. About half of the joiner is pushed onto the rail.

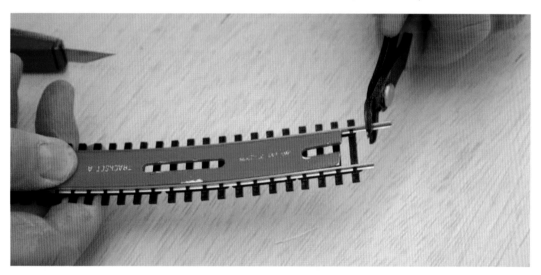

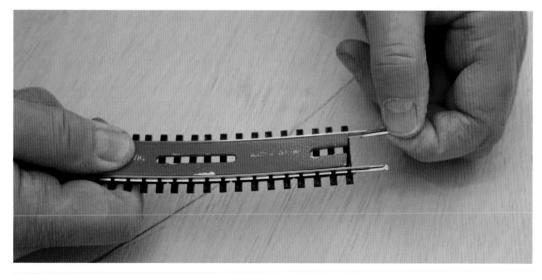

Left Stage 6: The curved track is now connected to the previous section and the rails pushed into the open ends of the joiners, making sure that the joiners slide correctly onto the bottoms of the rail on each side.

Below Stage 7: Continue using the Tracksetta gauge or follow the pencil line to maintain a constant curve, pinning the track through the centre of the Tracksetta as you go. The slots in the gauge assist pinning.

Stage 8: Trim off the plastic rail chairs from the previously removed sleepers.

Stage 9: Slide one or two of the trimmed sleepers into the gap underneath the rail joiners.

Stage 10: The completed section of track is laid with temporary track pins holding the curve and straight until any ballasting has been completed. Alternatively the pins can be carefully pushed fully in to hold the track as a permanent fixing option. Note that the two sleepers under the rail joint make the joint virtually invisible.

Points

The purpose of points (or turnouts as they are sometimes known) is to allow a train to change from one set of tracks to another. A train has no steerable wheels, so direction changing is carried out by the movable blades of the point swinging over from one side to the other and making direct contact with the rail on one side only. The flanges of the train's wheels are then guided by the inner face of the rails and subsequently the wheels and the train are sent in the direction selected by the closed and opposite open rails.

Some point terminology is explained in Figure 18. For ease of identifying the position of the point blades it is better to use the real railway term of 'normal' and 'reverse'. The normal route

is, in most cases, the straight ahead direction, unless the main line happens to be the curving route, in which case that would be the 'normal' side and the straight ahead direction would then become the 'reverse'. In Figure 18, if the main line is in the straight ahead direction the point is shown as reversed, as its reverse-side switch rail is closed against the fixed stock rail and trains will travel in the diverging (reverse) direction.

During track-laying where points are to be laid, thought should be given to how they are to be operated. If some form of electrical or mechanical operation of the point blades is to be used, now, before track-laying has been completed, is the time to consider how the operating mechanism will connect to the point. If it is to be below the baseboard, preparations need be nothing more than a suitably sized hole drilled centrally under the final position of the point's tie bar. Or if your chosen method is to fit electrically operated solenoid motors mounted directly onto the underside of the point's sleepers, such as that offered by the Peco system,

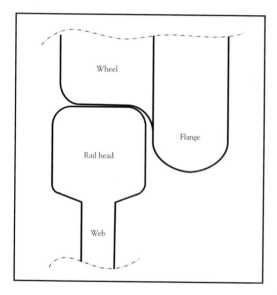

Left **Figure 17: The relationship of wheel flange to rail head**

Below **Figure 18: Point terminology. Always speak about points as if you are standing at the tip looking into the pointwork. In this example the right-hand switch rail is closed against the stock rail, allowing a train to use the left-hand junction track. The switch rails are held apart by tie bars (or stretcher bars), not shown here for clarity. In the model, the 'frog' (or crossing) may be of two types, insulated (Insulfrog) or live (Electrofrog). Always feed power to the points from the tip end – *never* allow power to be fed from the frog end to the tip.**

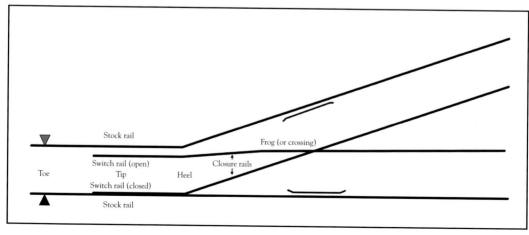

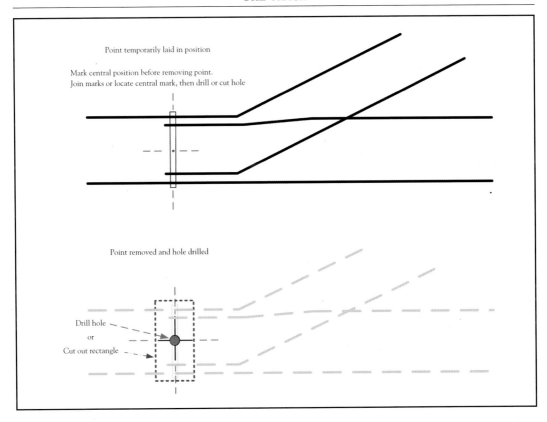

Point temporarily laid in position

Mark central position before removing point.
Join marks or locate central mark, then drill or cut hole

Point removed and hole drilled

Drill hole

or

Cut out rectangle

Above Figure 19: Peco or Hornby type point motor installation. The drawing shows the marking up of a typical point temporarily laid in its final position, but not fixed down. Where a point motor is to be used, fixed to the underside of the baseboard, or a mechanical method, such as 'wire in tube', a suitably sized hole needs to be drilled centrally under the tie bar of the point. Mark the tie bar's cross-track position on the baseboard, then hold the point blades centrally and mark the position of the drive-pin hole in the tie bar. Alternatively, pass a small drill bit through the centrally held tie bar to mark a small indent in the baseboard surface. Now remove the point and join up the marks as in the lower sketch, or identify where the indent is in the surface. Where the two lines cross, or where the indent is, marks the exact place a suitably sized hole needs to be drilled. For 'OO' this will be approximately 10mm in diameter; other gauges will need to be adjusted according to the amount of throw required to move the point from normal and reverse. Carefully remove any drill break-out swarf from the underside of the baseboard with the aid of a craft knife or a countersink drill bit.

Below A Peco Code 100 insulated (dead) frog double slip.

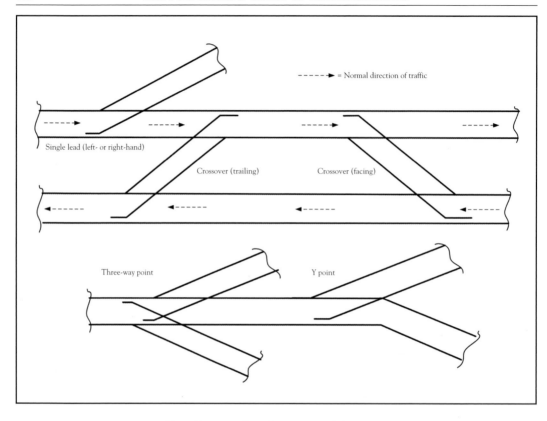

Above Figure 20: Some basic pointwork formations

Below A typical insulated (dead) frog diamond crossing.

a larger rectangular hole will need to be cut to accommodate the whole motor, use the centre-line as a guide; the rectangle will need to be approximately 40mm x 25mm. Note that in 'N' gauge you will need to offset the rectangular hole to one side depending on which way you have chosen to mount the motor onto the underside of the point. Figure 19 shows the procedure.

The hole is cut out of the baseboard by drilling four small holes (5-6mm) in each corner of the rectangle, then joining up the holes with the aid of either an electric jigsaw or a hand pad saw. After point-laying is completed, the hole will need to be covered over; thin card – postcard is ideal – is cut to approximately 50mm x 35mm, then cut in half lengthways. Next cut matching central slots some 10mm long and 3-5mm deep into one edge of each strip, and slide the strips into position under the point, perhaps securing them to the baseboard with the aid of a little paper glue; the slot should allow free movement of the operating pin in both directions.

Crossovers are made from two sets of single-lead points of the same 'hand', ie two left-hand or two right-hand points abutting, depending on the direction of the crossover. Some basic formations are shown in Figure 20. In addition, diamond crossings, single and double slips and scissor crossovers are available ready-made.

Ballasting

Ballast is the small stones used by the real railway to retain the track in position and prevent both sideways and sleeper-to-sleeper movement as a train passes over. For the modeller, the style of ballast representation is a personal choice between ready-made track sections with a ballast shoulder factory-moulded onto the track, foam inlay ballast, or real stone chippings.

The factory-moulded ballast shoulders on sectional pre-shaped track are perhaps the quickest way of track laying and giving a reasonable representation of real ballast. The only disadvantages I find are that the joint between each section of track does show markedly, and the overall appearance is often rather too much that of a 'toy' train set. Pre-ballasted track is available only in the smaller scales – 'N' and 'OO'/'HO' being the main two.

Foam inset strip ballast offers the modeller a longer run of continuous ballast representation, but will still have joints showing at points, diamond crossings and wherever the lengths of foam strips are abutted. Its main advantage is that it does offer a soft bed for the track to sit upon, which will help reduce sound levels. Track will require some light pinning down to prevent any movement, but the pins should only be lightly pressed through the sleepers and not actually push down the sleepers into the foam. One problem with some foam underlay is that after several years it may well start to crumble and need replacing.

Real stone is available in various grades and is often made from finely crushed granite. It is quite common to use the size for the next scale or gauge down, or the very finest size of product in the actual scale, for best representation of the real thing. In 'OO' scale I use a mix of 4 to 1 'N' scale ballast to fine 'OO'. Laid with the aid of a teaspoon acting as a shovel, the ballast is spread along the pre-pinned track, between and outside the rails. An artist's brush is used to tease the ballast into the final position, any surplus being either brushed forwards for later use or completely removed. Once the desired effect is achieved, spray the whole ballast area with a mist of water, with a tiny drop of washing up-liquid added – use an indoor plant mister or an empty and thoroughly washed-out cleaning liquid spray bottle. Next, using a 50/50 mixture of woodworking PVA glue and water, plus a tiny drop of washing-up liquid, in a small jar – bond the ballast into position. With the aid of a pipette or eye-dropper, drop the PVA glue and water mixture over the whole area to flood the ballast. The tiny drop of washing-up liquid in both the misting spray and the glue/water mixture allows the liquids to flow freely into the ballast, as it reduces the surface tension of the mixture.

Once the PVA glue mix has been used, don't move any of the ballast as you cannot correct errors at this stage. Also ensure that no glue can cause damage to anything under the layout, should it run out of any baseboard joints or wiring holes – which it will! After at least 24 hours, any surplus unglued ballast can be removed – the use of a vacuum cleaner is ideal.

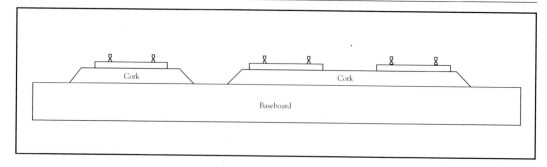

Figure 21: A cork underlay has been laid and trimmed, and the track fitted on top. The whole area is then covered in the appropriate ballast mix and glued in place.

For economy, most ballast can be reclaimed and reused later, so use a vacuum cleaner with a flexible pipe and place a stocking, popsock or cut-off tights leg inside the pipe, but firmly held on the outside of the tubing, to act as a 'catcher'. When the vacuum is turned off the stocking is pulled out of the tube and all the sucked-up ballast emptied out and reused. Some minimal retouching of the glued area is often necessary, where any ballast has not been fully bonded.

Some modellers use cork to raise the track above the baseboard surface to represent the full height of the ballast shoulder. In 'OO' this is often 2-3mm thick cork sheet, cut and laid a little wider than the sleepers' width and with the outer edges bevelled, so that the bottom is wider than the top – a cut of approximately 60 degrees is ideal (see Figure 21). Trim the cork with the aid of a sharp craft knife and a rule for straight runs, and cut to a drawn pencil line outside the sleeper edges on curves and pointwork. Once cut to shape, the cork will need to be glued to the baseboard with either PVA or an impact adhesive. Once dry, the track is then laid on top of the cork and lightly pinned in place. Stone ballast or other medium is glued in place depending on the effect required. Some areas will be representing a main line or a well-maintained loop or siding, while other areas may be, for example, at a coaling stage, where the track would have a considerable amount of fine coal dust mixed in with the ballast, or perhaps an ash drop area in a loco stabling siding, where the stone ballast could be replaced completely by

A section of track on the author's layout that has had the rail sides painted with a rusty colour to improve their appearance.

finely crushed ash. Once all the track and ballast has been securely glued and the glue fully set, any track pins can be carefully removed.

One alternative for very simple and easy ballasting is to use a 'ballast roll', as produced by, for example, Javis. This is simply rolled out, lightly glued with PVA adhesive over the whole track area and the track laid directly on top.

Weathering

Weathering of the rails, sleepers and ballast can be carried out at this stage, or, if preferred, the track and sleepers can be weathered prior to laying and the ballast used in the 'as supplied' colour. The use of an airbrush will be of help in applying the shades of track colour, though a large artist's brush can also be used.

Rust colour is applied to both sides of the rail and the top surface is then immediately wiped clean with a rag dipped in white spirit or turpentine to ensure that all paint traces are removed, as maintaining electrical contact with the locos is essential. Remember to mix tones of black, white and brown with the base red rust colour to add variety and realistic shading along the length of the track. Any paint that accidentally gets placed onto the rail chairs is left, as the chairs on the real railway are a rusty colour too. When weathering points, ensure the small area of the switch rail that touches the stock rail remains totally free of paint. A small strip of masking tape placed on the inside faces of the stock and switch rails will prevent accidental paint splashes, but remember to remove the tape as soon as painting has been completed.

5
THE LANDSCAPE

For the model railway to come to life there will be a need to reproduce the area surrounding the railway, usually including the area beyond the railway's boundary fence so that as a realistic perception is given to the viewer. The railway may run in open country, on embankments or in cuttings, and pass over bridges or viaducts where below runs a river or road. When the railway's fence line is reached we are taken into the open country, town, village, or industrial setting. Perhaps a mix of several of these is the ideal, with the train moving around and passing through open country then skirting an out-of-town industrial area with possibly a siding feeding a factory or gas works, before finally progressing to the actual town and station area. Some modellers may like to model just one scene, where perhaps a long terminus station and its approach tracks are depicted. The final choice is, of course, your own, and can be based on real places and buildings or be totally fictitious.

Cuttings, embankments and landscape effects

Cuttings and embankments are possibly the easiest to model. The sides can be made from either a scenic sheet of pre-coloured matting or, perhaps a little more realistically, by using plaster of Paris, plaster filler, plaster-impregnated bandage or even Artex ceiling texturing compound to mould the ground contours. All of these methods will require a foundation to give the basic shape to the embankment or cutting sides and offer a solid shape onto which to apply the final ground covering.

There are several ways of reproducing the base ground contours, including a framework of thick card, thin MDF or ply 'formers' cut to the basic shapes and glued in place, fine wire mesh similar to chicken wire, or even glued and carved polystyrene blocks. Card strips are my favoured method. Once the basic shape of the framework for the embankment or cutting is chosen, if required it is first filled with packing, such as crumpled newspaper or polystyrene. Next a grid of card strips is glued in criss-cross fashion over the base of crumpled newspaper or polystyrene to make the basic ground shape. If you are using wire mesh, cut and shape it, then pin or glue in place. I have found the use of a hot melt glue gun very useful for both card strips and wire mesh, as the glue rapidly sets and holds the strips or mesh secure.

The basic shape is then covered with plaster bandage, papier-mâché or a coarse cloth (such as that sold as mutton cloth for polishing) cut into strips and glued on with some diluted PVA glue, or perhaps a ready-made grass matting. Plaster of Paris, Artex or plaster filler, as preferred, is then spread over the dried sub-base. A brown earth colour, mixed from powder or acrylic paint, can if desired be added to the plaster when it is being mixed, as this helps prevent any white plaster patches later showing through the surface should it become chipped. This is particularly helpful on portable layouts where damage to the scenery is perhaps at times unavoidable.

As it dries the coating is carved or moulded with the aid of a spatula or spoon handle to give the required textured surface finish. Once dry (allow 24 hours) the surface can be painted with more brown ground colour and, when this has fully dried, a woodworking-type PVA glue is spread over the area and selections of scatter materials sprinkled on. Use several shades of the chosen colours freely intermixed. When this has finally dried, vacuum off all unstuck scatter using

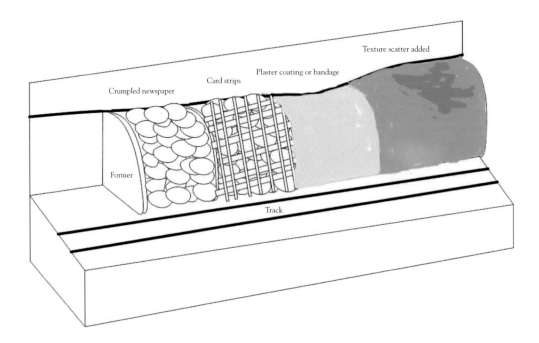

Figure 22: Basic construction techniques to form a cutting side. Where an embankment is to be modelled, the track is at the higher level and the scenic materials are taken down to baseboard level or even a little below where an open-top framing is being used.

the 'stocking in the tube' method (as described for ballasting) for reuse. Touch in any patches of scatter that may have come away and finally add bushes, trees and fencing to achieve the desired effect. The process is shown in Figure 22.

If you use polystyrene to make up the undersurface of the landscape, bond various thicknesses and shapes together using either woodworking PVA or special polystyrene adhesive. Place a weight on top of the structure to aid the gluing process. Once dried, carefully trim the polystyrene blocks to the required shape, using either a sharp craft knife or a hot wire cutter sold specifically for cutting polystyrene. One disadvantage of using polystyrene is the hundreds of tiny balls it produces when being cut, which spread everywhere and are quite hard to clear away! But, once covered with plaster or similar, it does make a very lightweight and solid structure.

If you are using the scenic sheeting, consider also adding some similarly coloured scatter to enhance the overall appearance of the slope. Use PVA woodworking glue spread over some of the

matting and sprinkle on the scatter as previously described, and again add further detailing such as fencing, trees and bushes. All these can be bonded on with neat PVA, which will dry clear. For fencing and bushes, apply a little drop of PVA around the base of the item after it has been glued in place and sprinkle on a tiny amount of reclaimed scatter material to blend it fully with the surrounding ground covering.

Rock or chalk cuttings can be modelled by using cork bark to represent a rock face. The cork, which is sold in packs containing several pieces, is simply glued in place until the required height and length is reached. Some green and brown scatter material mix is then PVA glued into the nooks and crannies of the rock face, and finally small clumps of lichen or similar are added to represent bushes clinging to the rock face. Chalk can be represented by thickly laid plaster, crack filler or Artex, which is then impressed with crumpled kitchen foil while still wet. Press the foil into the surface of the wet plaster, remove and add additional detail carved with the aid of a spoon handle or spatula.

Landscape construction in stages

Above Stage 1: Track-laying is under way. Note the tools being used: a steel rule to give a straight edge; a Tracksetta gauge to ensure that the correct radius or curve is maintained when using flexible track; a track spacing gauge (by Peco); long, curved-nosed pliers; Xuron rail cutters; craft knife; Archimedean drill with drill bit fitted; and a set of needle files. Where the steel rule is laying is the start of the slope leading up to the terminus station, which is to be at a higher level.

Below Stage 2: Basic track-laying has been completed and a DMU set is being used to test track alignment and electrical connections before moving on to ballasting the track and adding scenic details.

Above Stage 3: Thick mounting card has been covered with brick-effect paper to form retaining walls between the different track levels. These are downloaded printable files from Scalescenes.com, which, once paid for and downloaded, are printable as many times as the user wishes. The centre stretch of track has been ballasted. On the right note the large gaps in the sleeper spacing where two sections of flexible track abut; before ballasting, individual sleepers with their rail chairs removed will be slipped under the rails to fill the gaps. A small amount of basic ground scenic work has also been started. Once all the retaining walls are in place, they are given a coating of matt spray-on varnish from an aerosol can to help prevent them from absorbing any moisture from the track ballast and scenic gluing process.

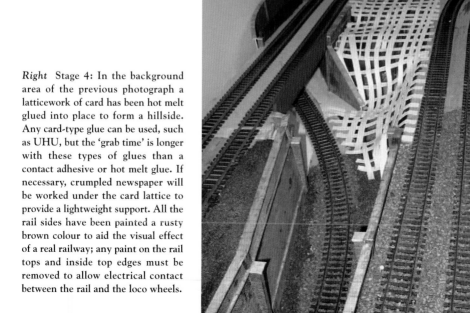

Right Stage 4: In the background area of the previous photograph a latticework of card has been hot melt glued into place to form a hillside. Any card-type glue can be used, such as UHU, but the 'grab time' is longer with these types of glues than a contact adhesive or hot melt glue. If necessary, crumpled newspaper will be worked under the card lattice to provide a lightweight support. All the rail sides have been painted a rusty brown colour to aid the visual effect of a real railway; any paint on the rail tops and inside top edges must be removed to allow electrical contact between the rail and the loco wheels.

Stage 5: Plaster-covered bandage, cut into small rectangles and soaked in a bowl of water for a few seconds, has been layered over the card lattice and carefully moulded before it sets to form a slightly uneven finish to represent the underlying ground shape. Placing some masking tape over the track and sleepers in the area prior to plastering will help prevent the sleepers becoming covered in white plaster, although once dried it comes off easily with the aid of a stiff brush. Once the plaster has fully dried, paint all the white areas with acrylic artist's paint. Use a dark brown colour, such as Burnt Umber, to represent the base soil colour. If desired, leave odd patches of white on sharp slopes to represent a chalk face.

Stage 6: Almost finished! Scatters in various shades of green with a base of earth brown and scenic clumps and foliage have all been PVA glued in place and the entire track has been ballasted. Rocky outcrops, as seen here to the right of the single line where the cutting rises to meet the ground above, can be modelled by using a suitable 'off white' scatter and blending it in with the surrounding earth and grass scatters. Signalling has been added (colour lights in this case) and some further scenic detailing has occurred in the field to the left of the main lines where 'Farmer Gates' is mending his tractor as the estate manager arrives to offer his help and advice! A Heljan *Falcon*, in lime green and chestnut prototype livery, heads an up train over the girder bridge. Only the field in the far corner and to the left of the passing train now requires added detailing.

More plaster can be added if the chalk face is not quite correct. As the chalk face will most likely be a white or off-white colour, when the plaster is dry a little additional painting will be needed, while some areas will need to be touched in to give the impression of dirtier chalk or even a little earth on the flat ledges. Add a little brown and green scatter mix to these ledges and perhaps also some lichen.

The chalk face on a more 'modern image' layout may have some anti-chalk-fall netting pinned over some of its surface. Don't forget that there will often be boulders of dislodged chalk laying at the base of the cutting from earlier falls, which the railway engineers will not move as they are not causing any problems to the trains or the track.

Farmland is produced by laying suitable earth- or grass-coloured matting or a scatter mix over a pre-glued area of the baseboard. Where a ploughed field is to be represented, corrugated cardboard can be cut and laid to the size required, then painted with artist's acrylic paints in a dark brown colour and lighter shades of brown near the tops of the furrows where the sun has dried the soil. The area is then covered with a glued-on mix of various brown scatters. Field edges are modelled to camouflage the join between field and baseboard; this can be a simple fence, a hedgerow or even a stone wall. Perhaps a scale tractor can be placed in the field or even some grazing sheep or cows in a field of grass to complete the scene. Don't forget the old weather-beaten tree in the corner!

Industrial scenes are quite simple to model, as they are normally all at the same level (the baseboard datum or on a raised sub-baseboard) and consist of brick, steel or concrete 'boxes' – actually more than that, as they need to detailed and shaped buildings. These can be scratch-built from card or plastic sheets or purchased as card or plastic kits; hundreds of kits are available to the modeller in virtually all the popular model railway scales, and many can be fairly easily altered to produce unique buildings by grafting two kits together, or not using all of one kit and adding some chosen details from similar matching materials.

Depending on the era being depicted, the industrial estate can be modern-day as a series of similar pre-fabricated buildings, or for the pre-1970s as two or three smaller units or one large 'works' – gasworks, brewery, dairy, single factory or a works producing … almost anything! These are just a few ideas of what is often found adjoining the lineside. Some will have a functioning siding, or, if in a more modern era, a disused siding serving the premises. Quite often the siding's entrance will be protected by a gate, similar to a wooden level crossing gate, normally shut across the siding and only opened when a goods train is due and is shunted in or out.

Towns will involve a lot more modelling work, depicting houses in single, semi-detached or terraced rows. Their fronts and backs may be shown, or they may be in half relief with just the front or rear of the building, perhaps with alleyways. Model shops and pubs, offices and even garages, both in lock-up blocks or singly belonging to a house, can be modelled. Roads, pavements, street signs and lamp posts are all major parts of the town scene, as are lots of people. Many kits of various styles of buildings are available, in both card and plastic, to help the constructor, and recently a supply of ready-made and painted items has become available, so the choice is huge. You can build your own buildings from card or plastic sheet or use a careful mix of both.

Buildings

You can scratch-build your own buildings to a detailed scaled plan of a real-life building or just something that is made up to fit a location. Card is perhaps the easiest material to work with and produces some fine buildings. It is usually clad with either brick or stone paper or with a plastic card; the latter will need painting to the desired finish. Building papers are produced by Superquick, Metcalfe and Scalescenes, to name but three of many, while plastic card is available from Wills, Evergreen and Plastikard in various scales. Ready-made buildings are produced by Hornby and Bachmann in 'OO' and 'N' scales and by several other producers in other scales.

To scratch-build a simple card building you will require some basic tools: a craft knife, ideally a scalpel type with a good supply of replacement blades (cutting card and paper quickly blunts knife blades); a steel rule for cutting straight edges; a small (3-4-inch) steel set square; a pencil; perhaps a self-healing cutting mat; plus, of course, a solid and firm surface on which to work. The choice of card needs to be considered, as some is manufactured with a twin thin wall, spaced apart by corrugation. I have not found this really suitable for buildings, preferring to use the card sold for making mounts for pictures. This is often available in A1 sizes and various colours, but I prefer plain white as this will not cause any 'show through' when finally covered with brick paper, if that is your chosen finish. The card is nominally around 2.5mm thick. Finally, you will need a suitable glue. UHU or a non-solvent-based impact adhesive is adequate, though some of these tube glues do produce a lot of 'stringing', which is a nuisance and should be kept off the finished model. PVA applied with a fine artist's brush, occasionally dipped in clean water to remove any residue PVA, is my overall choice for card modelling.

Commence by drawing onto the card in pencil the basic shapes needed – front, back and two sides, with gables if necessary. Use the set square to ensure all right-angles are true. Align the rule carefully on the pencil line and cut through the card with the scalpel, using several light strokes. Do not press too hard or try and cut through the card in one go. Keep your finger tips well inside the edge of the rule, and do not be tempted to use a wooden or plastic rule, as the knife blade will quickly cut into the edge and the rule will be useless. Next, draw onto the cut-out surfaces the window and door apertures, again using the set square to ensure that all is drawn square. If you are going to use ready-made windows or doors, perhaps from plastic, use these as a template and draw around them to obtain a tight or interference fit once the shape has been cut out.

To give the card model a realistic wall thickness, as seen at door and window openings, a simple little trick can be used on the model. Simply cut a piece of the same card a little larger than the finished opening and glue it onto the rear of the wall, covering completely the position of the previously cut out door or window. When the glue has dried, and using the steel rule and scalpel, cut through this backing card, carefully following the sides of the original aperture. This gives a double skin to the area of the aperture.

To strengthen the corners of your building, cut some small (approximately 12mm x 12mm) squares from spare card, then cut them diagonally into triangles, or fillets. Apply a continuous band of glue to one edge of the building's side and immediately butt this up to the adjoining wall. Keep the joint under light pressure until the glue grips the joint, all the time ensuring that the joint is kept true in all directions and that the bottom edges maintain a constant level in both directions. Now glue one or more of the triangular fillets to the inside joint to set the corner at an accurate 90 degrees. Set aside to allow the glue to dry fully, then proceed exactly the same with the other pair of walls.

Once the walls are dry and set, temporarily dry-assemble the four walls together and check, when lightly held together, that the structure is square and the walls all align correctly. Any discrepancies should be corrected at this stage by carefully removing any overly long wall sides to bring the structure back to square. Only when all is correct with the dry fix, apply two strips of glue to the two edges of each wall set and carefully assemble the complete structure into the basic box shape. Once the glue has grabbed the structure, add more of the triangular fillets to square it up and strengthen it. Make a final check for squareness, place to one side and leave for 24 hours.

Next, cut from card all the floors, including an internal base, any intermediate floors and a ceiling to fit on the top of the walls; use the actual building as the template and draw around the insides of the walls to give the correct size for all the floors. Apply glue to the four sides of the base floor and fit it into place flush with the bottom insides of the outer walls. Do not at this stage fit the intermediate or top ceiling boards.

Once the building has again been left to set fully, the next step is to produce the basic roof lining. Carefully measure the size of one of the roof side panels by measuring from the apex of the gable to the outer edge of the front wall and across the width of the two outer walls, then add a little to allow a small roof overhang over all three wall sides. The amount of overhang will

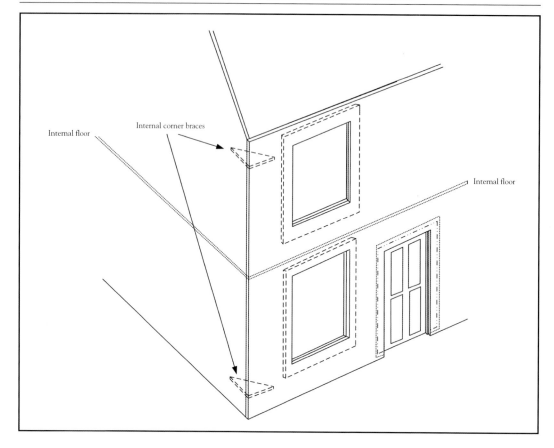

Figure 23: Basic card building construction. The door frame and door and window apertures are formed by gluing larger pieces of card behind the apertures and cutting out to the same size as the original openings.

depend on the scale being modelled; for 'OO'/'HO' 2-3mm is probably ideal on each side. Transfer these measurements to the card and cut out one roof section. Carefully measure the overall size of the other side of the roof using the first roof panel, held in place on top of the building, to give the correct measurements. Cut out this roof and in pencil mark this panel as the 'rear' section. It is now time to add the exterior cladding.

Paper cladding

If you are using brick or stone paper, apply with the aid of either ready-mixed wallpaper adhesive or PVA, spreading the glue onto the card wall, not the paper. Align the brick courses level with the bottom of the building and carefully press the paper onto the glued card, covering over any door or window apertures. Now lay the building, paper side down, on the cutting mat and, with a

new blade in the scalpel, carefully cut the paper along the edge of the wall. Pierce the window and door openings centrally, then, with the wall still laying face down on the cutting mat, carefully slit the paper from each of the four corners to the previously made central slit, making an X-shaped cut. Apply a little of the chosen paper adhesive all around on the inside of the aperture and also along the edges of the opening, then carefully fold each of the little 'X' flaps around the edges of the aperture and secure onto the insides of the wall. For doors only, bend over three of the flaps – only the top and two sides are glued into place around the aperture; the bottom flap is completely removed, if it has not already fallen off following the original cutting out of the 'X' shape. Turn the model over and do the same on the opposite wall, then set aside to dry.

When dry, apply adhesive onto one of the end

walls and apply the paper, checking that the brick or stone courses align around the corners and also run level along the bottom of the wall. When you are satisfied that all is correct, lay the newly papered wall, paper side down, on the cutting mat, and very carefully trim along the previously papered front and rear wall corner joints. Cut out as before any door or window apertures and glue back the flaps. Use artist's pastel sticks to tone in all edges and any small areas of bare card that may be showing; use the pastel colours directly or ground into a fine dust and applied with a fine-pointed brush as necessary.

Plastic cladding

If you have opted for a plastic cladding, lay the card building on the reverse side of the plastic card and, using a scalpel blade and starting in one corner, carefully draw around the wall, scribing the outline onto the card. Remove the building and gently, with the aid of the steel rule, continue to deepen the scored lines until finally the knife breaks through the embossed surface and the panel can be removed. Mark this cut panel and make a matching mark on the corresponding wall, eg '1' or 'A', and mark the top edge 'top'. Do the same with the remaining three walls, marking each with a unique identification number or letter and which edge is top. When all four panels have been cut, apply the chosen adhesive to one wall. Most modellers like to use an impact adhesive to bond the plastic to the card, but do test a small amount of the glue on a scrap piece of the plastic to ensure that it doesn't cause any wrinkling or other unwanted effect on the plastic. Spread the glue over the wall surface and bond on the plastic. Carefully trim off any overhangs by laying the wall face down on the cutting mat and trimming along the card/plastic edge. Continue by gluing the remaining three sides in place, ensuring that the 'top' mark is maintained throughout! Trim any overhangs as before. Cut out door and window openings in the same way as for trimming the overhangs. If wished, slivers of embossed plastic card can be cut and glued into the window and door reveals.

If the chosen plastic is one of the thicker sizes, eg Wills card, there is often no need to produce a card backing, as the plastic sheets will be self-supporting. However, on the corners it will be necessary to chamfer all corner joints to approx 45 degrees inwards – which means that each panel has to be cut over-size to allow for this! Gluing plastic to plastic is quite straightforward and I recommend the use of one of the liquid types of solvent glues such as Slaters Metpak or Humbrol Liquid Poly. These liquids are applied to the joints, whenever possible on their inner faces, thereby preventing any accidental glue damage to the surface of the finished model. Simply hold together the two parts to be bonded and run an old artist's brush, dipped in the liquid solvent, along the length of the joint, applying a little more if the area being brushed is on the long side. The liquid solvent flows under capillary action into the joint and causes the two plastic surfaces to melt and bond together. Carefully place the two joined parts to one side to allow the joint to dry fully and become solid; this may take several hours depending on the plastic and the solvent used. Often other pieces of the construction can be completed while these joints dry. When using solvent glues always ensure that there is adequate fresh air entering the room, as the fumes emitted are quite harmful. I recommend standing the bottle of solvent in an old coffee mug or use a large lump of Blutack or similar on the base of the bottle to prevent it accidentally being knocked over – it is sure to fall over and run everywhere if you don't try to prevent it!

Finishing off

Once the basic shell is complete, add any internal wall decoration as required, then glue into place the door and windows, which, if plastic, have previously been painted and are thoroughly dry. Plastic windows can have some clear acetate sheet carefully glued over the inside to represent glazing. Now glue in place any intermediate floors and the ceiling panel, having firstly painted the flooring to a chosen colour. If internal details are required such as curtains, furniture or people, these should be added before the appropriate intermediate or ceiling panels are fitted. Finally glue the two roof panels into place, ensuring that the ridge of the roof is kept tightly joined and runs straight. Add the chosen

Above A road overbridge, with the station booking office building on top, is shown under basic construction. The station building is still removable but has been laid in place to check dimensions. The card used is mounting card and the structure will be covered in brick paper.

Below The same bridge and building are now virtually complete, with some further small detailing still to be undertaken.

roof finish, which might be tile or slate paper, plastic card, or individually cut tiles or slates from card or plastic, laid on from the bottom edge up and each row overlapping the previous one a little.

When painting buildings, wherever possible use a matt finish paint. The reason for this is that, if you looked at a real building from around 250 feet away, which is roughly equal to the scale distance from which you are viewing the model at approximately 3 feet away, the distance causes the gloss of the paint to appear matt or semi matt – thus a matt paint finish on the model will add that little extra to the realism. If you are using oil-based paints, such as those in the Humbrol range, and there is no matt finish available, I recommend the use of a little talcum powder mixed into the gloss paint and thoroughly stirred. The talc absorbs and removes most of the gloss – but do not overdo the talc or you will end up with an unworkable sludge! Mix a little and try the mixture on a scrap piece of plastic – you can always add a little more if need be, but it is impossible to remove any that has been over-mixed! Use a high-quality artist's brush to apply the paint; skimping with brush quality will result in brush lines showing. Always allow at least 24 hours between coats and, if possible, place the painted model in a dust-free area to dry – an airing cupboard is ideal. Place the model in an old shoe box or similar to prevent any dust falling or being blown onto the wet paint.

Whenever possible apply light colours first, followed by darker ones. However, where brick or dark stonework is being represented, the base colour is often needed first, eg a brick red. This base colour may at times be darker than the colours used to highlight the various shades of individual bricks or stone blocks, which are later picked out individually. Once the base colour has fully dried and the individual stones or bricks have been painted in and dried, use a technique called 'dry brushing' to lightly wipe over the base coat, infill any small areas and bring out the highlights. Often a dirty wash of colour is used for this, mixing black, grey and a little white until a grimy colour is reached. To dry brush, dip the tip of a clean brush into the paint and immediately wipe off 90-95% of the paint with a clean tissue. Then very lightly wipe the now almost dry brush over the surface to be highlighted. What little paint the brush transfers will deepen very slightly the surface colour and cause a more realistic appearance on the model than if left in the base colours.

Finally, add details such as gutters, downpipes, waste or soil pipes serving bathrooms or toilets, door canopies – perhaps on older buildings the external wall tie plates often seen as 'S' shapes at intermediate floor level, and a road name if the building is on a corner. Chimney stacks, both side and centrally located, and their pots can be added as required. Finely detailed parts, some as described, can be obtained from good model shops, and are made from plastic or a brass etching. Remember, it is those little details that make the model stand out from the rest!

Bridges and tunnels

These commonly form part of a model railway. A bridge might carry a road over the railway, or the railway over a road, another railway, a river or stream. They normally have brick, stone or concrete abutments, and the bridge span will be made from steel plate girders, concrete beams or brick or stone arches – perhaps even a mixture of two in one bridge length, as is sometimes seen. They can be very short in length – such as, for example, a narrow underpass or 'cattle creep' used by a farmer as a means of moving cattle from one field to another, or where a culvert is required to drain the land into a stream. Much longer and normally taller bridges are usually termed viaducts; these are normally a multi-arched crossing of a river, or are used where low-lying land is far below the level of the line, which is running above on embankments. Many ready-made bridges are available, as well as kits, while for scratch-builders sections of bridges are readily available to enable them to produce good and realistic examples. Some kits allow the constructor to alter the basic configuration and produce a unique bridge suitable for a particular purpose.

Again, the use of card and either brick or stone papers or embossed plastic card is a good way of producing either a complete arched bridge or just the abutments to support the chosen type of span. Metal girder spans, usually

A plate girder bridge on the author's layout.

made in plastic by suppliers such as Peco, Ratio and Wills, are sold for use in most gauges.

A tunnel likewise requires a reason to be there – the surrounding land should slowly rise from the baseboard datum to above the height of the tunnel portal. Usually a cutting precedes a tunnel, where the real railway builder started digging out the surrounding land for the railway until the cutting became too deep and a tunnel became the only option. Full-size tunnelling was an extremely expensive and time-consuming option to undertake and would be avoided whenever possible.

The entrance to a tunnel is called a 'portal' and is normally made from brick or stone, spanning one or two tracks. Most tunnel portals have side walls, or 'wing walls', retaining the ground around the tunnel entrance. The inside of the tunnel is not always perfectly circular in shape, but is more often elliptical, with shallower sides and a more curved roof. Not all tunnels are fully brick or stone lined internally, and some

only have a few feet of wall clad in brick, the rest being substrate of rock or chalk itself. Of course, on the model most of the internal area will need to be painted a matt black to represent the darkness of the tunnel, and only the first couple of inches or so need be covered with brick or stone paper or embossed plastic card. Many ready-made tunnel portals are available, and some produced in kit form. Modellers can also make their own in the same fashion as bridge abutments, by using card with brick or stone paper or plastic card covering.

Avoid the 'train set' ready-made tunnel which is extremely unrealistic and looks like a hillock stuck in the landscape!

Remember to arrange adequate and easy access to the inside of the tunnel, as it is an unwritten law that the train will derail or fail somewhere inside, and you will need to be able to reach it. There is of course also a need to clean the rails in the tunnel. Access can be from the back, underneath or via a lift-off top scenic section.

A single-track line entering a tunnel portal.

Roads, vehicles and people

Roads will probably need to be modelled to serve our countryside, and certainly in industrial areas and towns. These can be made from thin card or, as I prefer, 2-3mm MDF sheet cut to the profile of the required area. If the road surface is tarmac, paint it in a medium to dark grey matt, then add shades of darker grey nearer the road edges and centre line where traffic doesn't normally run. White lines or road markings, if needed, can be reproduced by using thin strips cut from self-adhesive paper such as that used for printer labels. However, I have found that road markings tend to turn a fairly realistic scene into a toy, so use with care and only if really necessary. Pavements are not always seen in industrial or countryside areas, but can be modelled. There are several manufactures of card and plastic sheets replicating pavements and kerb stones, so there is little point in trying to scribe thin wet plaster into paving slab shapes, as eventually it will probably crack and look poor anyway.

When laying pavements ensure that your buildings actually sit inside the pavement. This gives the building the correct appearance of being there before the pavement was laid rather than the building sitting on top of the pavement and looking as though it has just been dropped there.

Try to place scale-sized road vehicles in realistic poses on the model road. I try to avoid having vehicles turning a corner, as they never look quite correct. Placed them as if they are about to turn the corner or enter a junction, or just after the corner or junction and have already straightened. Add scale people to the pavements, or the factory yards in the industrial complex. Pose them in a small group of two to three talking together, waiting for a bus or about to move an object, as well as a few just walking along doing their own thing!

People in suitable scale sizes can be obtained

Above A scene from the author's former layout showing people placed in realistic poses.

Left A set of ready-painted 'OO' modern track-worker figures. *Courtesy of and © copyright Bachmann Europe Ltd*

as either ready painted or as unpainted plastic or white metal castings, which are then painted in your own choice of colours. Always use a matt paint for clothing, and do remove the 'block of concrete' some plastic figures have on their feet! Use a new scalpel blade to carefully slice the figure's shoes away from the moulded base, then use superglue to hold them in place on the pavement or wherever they are to be placed; alternatively, drill a fine hole up through one foot into the figure's leg, then glue a sewing pin into the hole and cut off the pinhead. Drill a similar-sized hole in the location where the figure is to stand and place the pin into the hole, ensuring that the figure's foot or shoe is correctly down onto the ground.

6
ELECTRICAL

Normally, model railways operate on safe low-voltage power supplies, typically 12-volt direct current (dc); some other types run at 24-volt dc or 12-volt alternating current (ac), but these are in the minority. Some use mains-powered power supplies, which safely reduce the input voltage to the low voltage needed and, where necessary, convert the mains power from ac to dc, while others use on-board batteries, often rechargeable, to power the loco motors. Digital Command Control (DCC) has also now taken a strong hold.

Firstly a word of warning: *never allow mains power (230v ac in the UK) to go anywhere on the baseboard. If mains voltage is allowed onto the baseboard there is a very serious risk of electrocution and possible death.* Only safe low voltage should be used here. Mains supplies and all the associated transformers should be housed in commercially made or expertly produced enclosures, which should either be 'floor' or 'off-layout' mounted. Umbilical cables or individual wires then supply the appropriate safe and low voltages to the layout. The only exception to this rule is where a commercially made controller with a built-in transformer requires a direct mains input; this will normally be via a suitable flexible mains cable, often permanently fitted into the controller's casing, though some controllers employ the use of a 'kettle' or computer-style mains plug and socket for the mains input connection. Both of these types are safe and no other action is required other than the occasional inspection of the mains cable and any plugs for possible damage. Any damage noted should immediately render the cable or unit unusable until a professional repair is undertaken or the unit is replaced.

Control equipment

The **transformer** (isolating transformer) is the means by which ac mains electricity is converted from a high to a lower voltage. (The reverse is also possible, ie low to high voltage, but this isn't normally used on a model railway.) Transformers are available in many guises; they are sold as plug-in units, free-standing units with one or two cables connecting into them (normally the mains input cable and low-voltage output leads), or sold as a totally encased unit. There is one other type which needs expert safe installation, and this is known as an 'open' or uncased transformer, which can be purchased from many specialist suppliers such as Gaugemaster. All the above are merely transformers – they offer no actual control of the trains, but simply reduce the ac mains power to the required safe low voltages used on the model railway.

The **rectifier** is a device used to convert ac current into dc current. Most model railway power supplies will have at least one full-wave (bridge) rectifier fitted into their low-voltage supplies to provide a dc power source. Modern full-wave bridge rectifiers used for model railways are made from four 'rectifier diodes'. Diodes can be likened to a one-way valve for the flow of electrons or electricity – the current will pass one way through the diode but is prevented from flowing back the other way. Often bridge rectifiers are factory encased in a plastic moulded block, and have four connection terminals or wires on the casing; two are the ac input connections marked normally as either 'ac' or with a wave form symbol ($\sim$). The two dc output terminals are marked as + (positive) and – (negative).

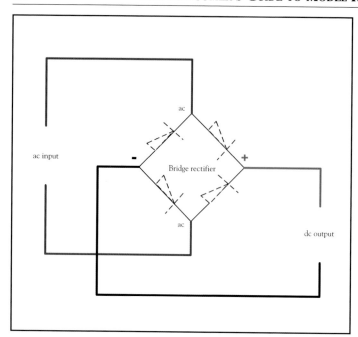

Left Figure 24: A bridge rectifier circuit

Above A bridge rectifier. The chamfered corner on the body is the dc positive connection and is denoted by the engraved + symbol.

The full-wave rectifier produces a reasonable, but unsmoothed, dc at its output terminals, which is ideal for most model railway applications. A bridge rectifier circuit is shown in Figure 24. The diagram shows how the alternating current (ac) flows from its supply into the bridge rectifier, then, via the four diodes, passes out as a dc supply. How is this achieved? When the ac frequency on the supply wires is at positive on the upper wire (negative on the lower) the positive current flows into the bridge and is blocked by the upper left diode. However, it can flow via the upper right diode out to the dc positive wire. The dc negative then returns via the black dc wire into the bridge rectifier and can then flow back to its ac negative source via the lower left diode. The ac supply changes polarity, so now the positive side of the ac cycle is on the lower input wire. It now flows via the lower right diode to reach the dc side's positive wire. The negative dc, still on the black wire, returns to its ac negative via the upper left diode. Remember that the ac supply is changing polarity at some 50 times a second in the UK (60 times a second in some other parts of the world), and this is known as the ac frequency, or Hertz.

Simpler, half-wave, rectification can be produced by using just one diode wired into one ac supply's path. Unfortunately the output is a very rough formation of the direct current needed and actually has only 50% of the total ac frequency turned into the dc form. For example, where a 50Hz ac supply is converted via a single diode, only half of the 50Hz (half-wave) is allowed to pass through the diode, therefore the output can be considered as being switched on and off 50 times every second. It is therefore very limited in its application.

The **controller** is next in the line of train control. Here we will find many variants, but basically they are all doing the same job. They take a specified low-voltage input, which is often 16 volts ac (from the transformer), and usually convert it to dc via a built-in rectifier. Some desk-style controllers have built-in transformers, such as the Hornby HM2000 or the Gaugemaster 'Model D', while others have a mains plug-in transformer and a low-voltage cord to feed the controller. Some, only have a 16-volt ac input, and these are normally panel mounting or hand-held versions. The output from the controller is referred to as the 'controlled' supply, as turning up the controller's knob increases output while turning it down reduces it. From the controller's 'controlled' output we take this supply to the rails and power our trains.

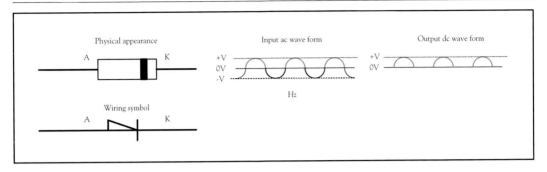

Figure 25: A typical diode and its wiring symbol, and how the ac and dc wave forms would look: note the outputs missing half cycles or Hertz (Hz). The symbols 'A' and 'K' refer to the Anode and Cathode (positive and negative) connections (note that the letter 'K' is used for the word Cathode!).

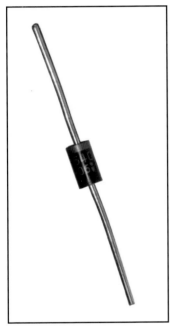

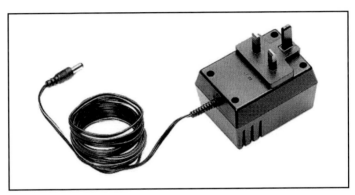

Above A typical diode. The silver-banded end is the Cathode (negative) connection.

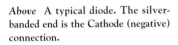

A Hornby plug-in mains transformer (*top right*), a low-voltage train controller (*middle right*), and the Hornby HM2000 twin-track controller with built-in transformer (*right*). *Photographs courtesy of and © copyright Hornby Hobbies Ltd*

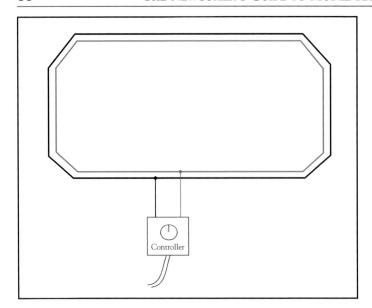

Figure 26: The basic train set

Some controllers will offer more than one output, especially where a mains transformer is built in. Typically on a single-knob transformer controller there will be one 12-volt dc controlled output, one 12-volt dc uncontrolled and one 16-volt ac uncontrolled output, or at times just one of the latter two. The controlled output is used to power the track, while the 12-volt uncontrolled dc can be used to feed a second controller or power accessories such as lighting for buildings. The 16-volt ac output can feed a hand-held controller or, more normally, is used to provide power to operate solenoid-style point motors, perhaps via a Capacitor Discharge Unit (CDU) and momentary contact lever or toggle switches – more of that later.

The basic train set controller is often a single controller feeding a simple loop of track, as shown in Figure 26. Adding a second loop means that a second controller is required, and this is shown in Figures 27 and 28, with insulated and live frogs points respectively. Note that the two controllers can be either two separate units or a dual controller having two separate control knobs in a single case.

Wiring diagrams and track plans

It is at this stage that consideration needs to be given to how the final layout will operate. Will

there be just one operator, or more? Will one or more control panels or, if you decide not to use a custom-made control panel, controller locations be required? Let us assume that one control panel has been decided upon, with provision for one or two operators, though one person could operate the layout single-handedly if need be.

First draw out your track plan, then start to consider where track power feeds will be required and where isolating sections need to be installed. Remember on dc systems always to try and feed the track power into a set of points from the tip or switch rail end, never from the frog direction. When using live-frog (what Peco terms 'Electrofrog') points you must install two rail isolating breaks, one in each rail, ideally at the rail ends after the frog on the two vee rails. Do

Above right Figure 27: The basic twin controller and track feed wiring. Note that a section of the inner siding track has an insulated rail joiner (IRJ) fitted into one rail joint. This joiner allows the section of rail beyond the joiner towards the buffer stops to be switched off or on (isolated or energised) as required to hold a loco electrically isolated from the remainder of the tracks. All the points in this drawing are of the insulated frog type.

Right Figure 28: This is the same layout with live-frog points. Now the insulated rail joiners (IRJs) will have to be fitted into the ends of the vee rails leading away from the point frogs, and the rails beyond the IRJs will require additional track feed wires to be connected to them. In this case an additional ten IRJs and four extra wires are required.

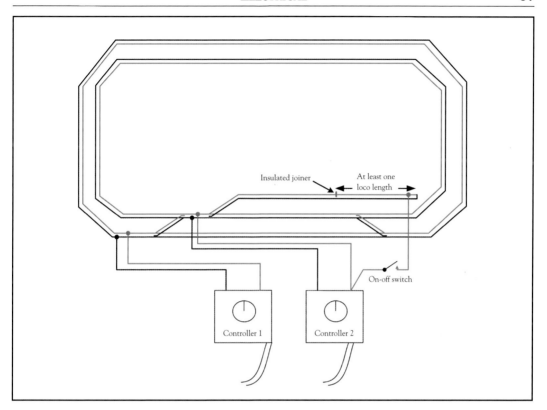

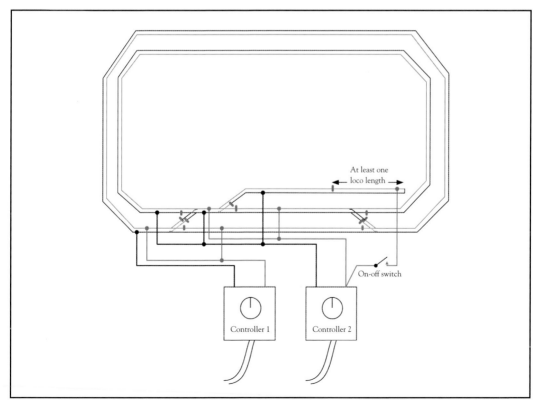

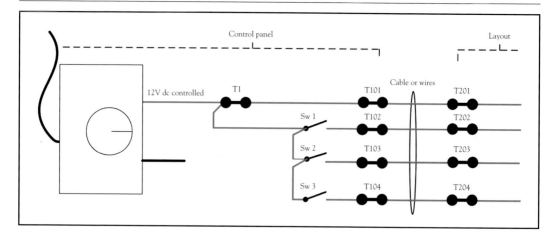

Above Figure 29: Wiring diagrams can be as simple as the example shown here. In this case, one of the controller's two output terminal wires is shown feeding three isolating switches and one direct rail track feed. As the wiring passes around the layout there is a need for terminals, and these are shown as 'dumb-bell' symbols representing the two sides of the screw terminal block; each black circle represents a connection on one terminal block. On a portable layout there would also be plug and socket pins to be shown to allow cross-board connections. Each item is uniquely labelled to aid future wire tracing or fault-finding. Sixteen lengths of wire, three switches and nine terminals are shown in all – note that the switches are drawn as 'open' (isolated or 'off').

Below Figure 30: Track plans need to be kept reasonably simple, yet still fully represent the whole layout. Shown here is a single-track railway operated as a continuous run, with one passing loop for the station platform and three sidings. Electrical track feeds are shown by the triangles – solid red are positive feeds, solid black are the return or negative connections, while isolating section feeds are shown as yellow triangles. Insulated rail joints are shown in each rail as required. It will be noted that there are two track feeds, 1 and 2 (red triangles), along the lower section of the track, but only one black return connection. This is because the actual loop of track on the red rail is isolated by two insulated rail joiners in the platform area and another set at the top – in the latter case both rails are fitted with insulated joiners. All points provide track power switching for the direction set.

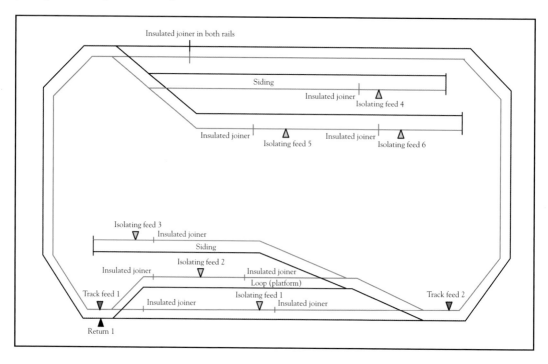

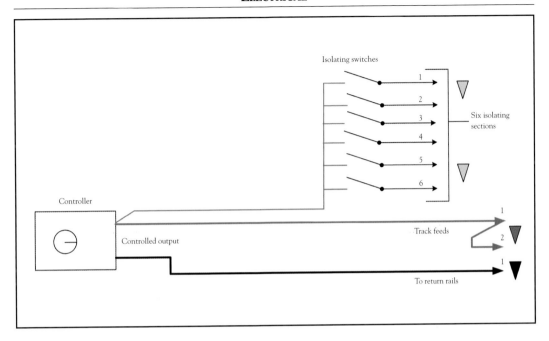

Above Figure 31: The track feed wiring diagram for the track plan shown in Figure 30

Below Figure 32: Part of a real track plan from a former layout. Note the use of unique series of numbers for the down-line track feeds (100 series) and up-line track feeds (200 series), together with the introduction of point numbering; the 'normal' position of the points is shown by a letter 'N' on the switch blade side, which is closed for the route chosen as 'normal'. The blue triangles are track feeds controlled by signal aspects: a signal at red means that the track feed is off, while at yellow or green the track feed is restored. As all the points are live frog, there is a need to install more insulated rail joints, hence the red lines shown cutting across the rails. All this information helps with pre-planning, track installation, wiring and any later alterations or fault-finding.

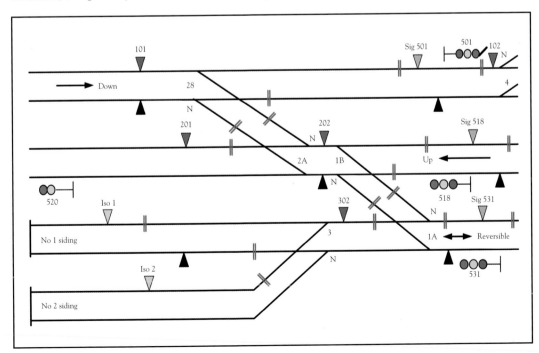

the same wherever a supply feed rail meets a return rail. Don't forget that on a loop you should always insert a rail break in the rails at both ends of the loop, as this prevents any electrical short circuit problems. If you are using insulated-frog points such as Hornby or Peco Setrack, or the latter's Streamline 'Insulfrog' versions, the need for insulated joiners is greatly reduced, as the frog switches the rail power, ie only the track to which the point is set is powered. The other direction is isolated until it is selected as the required route, then the first track becomes isolated. Consider how you may wish to switch certain sections of track between two or more controllers, making a 'cab control' system.

Wiring diagrams and track plans can be ignored for layouts that are little more than a basic oval of track. However, for anything larger they are virtually a must. They need not be overly complex and need be little more than pages in a note book. However, for full reference a nicely drawn and annotated wiring sheet and track plan book is the perfect reference for later fault-finding or alterations to circuits.

What should be in this book? Well, the basic track plan is ideally drawn as two lines representing the two rails, and all points and crossings are shown. Onto the track are marked the electrical feeds (positive and negative), all insulated rail joiners, and any isolating section feeds. Additionally signals can be depicted. Every track feed is given a sequential number, as are all the point ends. Isolating section feeds are given a different series of numbers, to show the main electrical feeds. If you choose to run coloured wires for certain functions, these colours should be shown too. Any terminal blocks used should be clearly shown, together with the actual terminal number used for each circuit; basically, one drawn line represents the actual piece of wire on the layout. Examples of wiring diagrams and track plans are shown in Figures 29 and 30, while the actual track feed wiring diagram for the simple plan shown in Figure 30 is given in Figure 31. Part of an actual track plan from one of my former layouts is shown in Figure 32.

The track and wiring plans could be produced on a computer or if preferred on plain paper with the aid of a rule and some coloured pencils – there is nothing really high-tech about them. I use a ring binder to store all my sheets, as they change far too quickly!

Common return

Common return is where all track and accessory electrical return paths are fed into one – common – wire. Every return path is connected together, then one or more (if need be) return wire(s) go back to one or all of the appropriate controller's output terminals for all supplies – ac and dc. The reason this method is chosen is its simplicity of wiring and the reduced number of wires needed to get everything back to the controllers and PSUs. There are, of course, other methods of wiring, and by no means is 'common return' better than any other. Other methods of return include giving each return its own direct wire path, but this is hugely wasteful on wiring. Another alternative is to consider splitting returns to, say, all track power supplies, all point power, all signalling, all lighting and everything else – ie up to five return paths. There is no advantage in this over the conventional one-wire common return system.

One thing that must be certain before the common return can be used is that each low-voltage power outlet or supply and its return originates from a totally separate winding on the transformer or separate transformers. One winding feeding two outputs or controllers with a common return wire linking their connections will result in a certain short circuit, and this type of supply cannot be used for common return. A simplistic overview of how a common return system is wired is shown in Figure 33. Note that all the supplies are from separate transformers or separate windings on the same transformer. Then one output terminal from each supply is linked (or common connected) to the next, and finally a heavy-gauge wire is taken onto the layout for all circuit returns to connect to. The dc and ac supplies are intermixed and all work happily together.

Roughly in the middle of each baseboard, or approximately every 3-4 feet (900-1200mm) on a longer baseboard, place a common return 'bus bar' connection. This need be nothing more than a

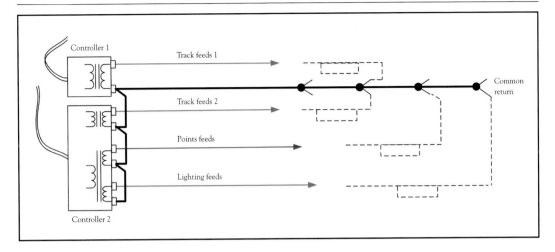

Above Figure 33: A simple diagram showing how a common return system is wired. The dotted rectangles and lines represent the various loads applied to the circuit, eg loco motors, point motors, lamps for street or station illumination and building lighting, etc.

Below Figure 34: A common return bus bar connection

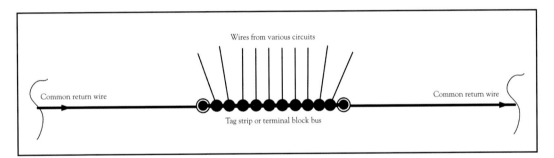

Right A two-way terminal block used as a common return bus connection point. The common return wiring is seen entering and leaving on the right, while on the left is a copper link or bus wire, which links the incoming and outgoing common return wires. Onto this linking wire are soldered the local return wires from the rails, point motors, signals, layout lighting, etc. The copper link or bus wire is also a suitable and easy accessible place to connect the fly lead of a multimeter or other testing device to enable testing and checking of circuits.

piece of single tag strip or two terminal connector blocks with a length of bare wire (1mm copper domestic wire is ideal) linking the two terminals. The common return wire arrives at one terminal of the common connection, then the electrical path is via the copper bus wire to leave again via the opposite tag or terminal, leading to the other sections of the layout, or to the next board if it is a portable layout. The electrical returns from that baseboard or section of baseboard are soldered onto the copper wire of this common return bus bar, as shown in Figure 34.

Types of wire

Wire used on the layout should ideally be of a flexible type for all electrical work, nominally $7/0.2mm^2$, $16/0.2mm^2$, $24/02mm^2$ and $32/02mm^2$; the latter two are often used for common return wiring, which may be kept in a black coloured wire sheath. The description '$7/0.2mm^2$', for example, signifies the number of copper wire strands inside the PVC insulation or sheath (7) and the actual size of each of these individual wire strands ($0.2mm^2$). Thus '$16/0.2mm^2$' has 16 individual wire strands inside its insulation covering, and so on. The colour of the sheathing really does not matter, whether red, green, blue or yellow, etc; you can use all one colour or decide to make the wires colour specific, eg red for all track feeds, blue for all point feeds, etc. $7/0.2mm^2$ wire can carry nominally 1.4 amps, so it is ideal for most model railway wiring on 'N' gauge and, in some situations, 'OO' gauge, while its larger brother, $16/0.2mm^2$, can carry at least 3.0 amps and is suited to the larger gauges ('O', 'G', etc). $16/02mm^2$ is also ideal for 'N' and 'OO' point motor wiring, or on small layouts as a common return wire, where at any one time there might be 2-3 amps flowing. On larger layouts consider using $24/02mm^2$ for point motor feeds, $16/02mm^2$ for track feeds and a common return wire of $32/02mm^2$ or $50/02mm^2$ to allow for the overcoming of any voltage drop and, of course, increased current flow.

The use of solid single-strand wire should really be avoided. In the main this is the so-called 'Post Office'-style wire (former telephone cable wire) or bell wire. While it will work, it breaks far too easily, suffers severe voltage drop due to its small size, thus reducing its current-carrying capability, and is certainly not suitable for any layout that is portable. So stick with the flexible types. Cable sold for burglar alarm installations is sometimes a good choice; it is normally sold in 4, 6, 8 or more cores in one cable sheath and has flexible conductors often of the $7/0.2mm^2$ size. It is ideal for bringing indications back to the control panel or operating colour light signals, etc.

If your layout is of a medium to large size, say more than 10ft x 6ft 6in (3m x 2m), consider carefully at the planning stage what size all the control circuit wires need to be, and allow a margin of error, opting for the next larger size if need be. If problems are encountered after wiring, such as solenoid point motors failing to throw every time, you can always double-up the problem circuit wires; this will help overcome any volt-drop problems and also give more current flow potential.

How to wire a layout

As previously mentioned in the section on baseboards, I recommend drilling 15-20mm-diameter holes roughly centrally into all the cross bracing timbers below the baseboard. This will allow ample wire-running access, will ease wire installation, and keep the wiring out of the way. The use of 'zip' cable ties to bunch the individual wires into looms also makes for very neat wiring. As mentioned previously, for all common return paths it is recommended that you use at least the $16/0.2mm^2$ wire or larger in a black colour. Run this in first, then follow it with all the track feeds (in, say, red wire), marking them onto the wiring diagram as they are run in and terminated. Use identification 'tags', made from masking tape wrapped around the individual wire to form a U-shaped tag; write any details on this tag and only remove it when all has been tested and found correct.

Solder tag strips are ideal for terminating wiring at each baseboard's end where portable layouts are being used – there is nothing like a nice strong soldered joint! I personally dislike, but have to use through sheer economics, the nylon twin-grub-screw terminal strips (12-way plastic blocks with two grub screws per termination) as these have a tendency, when the grub screw is tightened down, to cause the wire end to break off due to the tension and twisting motion placed on the stripped wire end. There are some blocks that have a flexible metal strip directly under the grub screw, which presses down onto the wire as the grub screw is tightened. This type is fine but is very hard, if not near impossible, to find in most electrical stores. Soldering, or 'tinning', the wire end before inserting it into the terminal block does help prevent the twisting/snapping action on the stripped wire end.

These two 25-way 'D' connectors are being used on a semi-permanent layout where occasionally the connections and boards need to be parted. Thus the plug-and-socket configuration is of the in-line type. Coloured insulating tape helps ensure quick and correct coupling, as does the unseen fact that on each side of the joint the 'D' connectors comprise plugs and sockets in opposite male/female configurations.

On portable layouts, where inter-baseboard connections are needed, or on a fixed layout where perhaps a removable control panel is required, the use of computer-style 'D' connectors as multi-way plugs and sockets is recommended. These are available with nominally 9, 15 and 25 ways, but larger versions are also available. Using the male and female halves of a 'D' connector you can produce either in-line joints, or one side can be permanently mounted on the baseboard or control panel, allowing its mating half to be connected via an umbilical-type flexible cable or single cores of wire made into a bundle. When more than two 'D' connectors are required, mark each one with different-coloured tape or paint and also reverse each connection, so that a male plug has a female socket next to it, as this also helps to prevent incorrect accidental cross-connections.

When removing the insulation from the end of a wire, use a pair of specially made wire strippers, as these will remove the insulation without damaging the fine strands of copper wire inside. Alternatively, and only with practice, use wire side cutters. Never use your teeth! You only get one adult set and your dental practice will not appreciate you appearing with a tooth missing or a notch cut into the enamel!

Soldering

There is only one way of making a solid electrical connection as far as I am concerned, and that is by soldering! People shy away from soldered connections and I can never really understand why. The basic requirements are a soldering iron of suitable wattage for the work being undertaken, fitted with a clean bit in good condition; rosin-cored solder; and clean connections. For everyday soldering a 25-watt iron with a small to medium bit is all that is

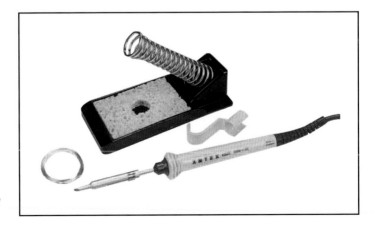

A soldering iron and stand. *Courtesy of and © copyright Maplin Electronics*

required. Larger bit sizes and higher-wattage irons have their place, but not for most electrical joints. I use mainly two soldering irons, a 25-watt and an 18-watt Antex; both do an identical job, but the smaller-wattage one has a 1mm-diameter tip fitted while the 25-watt one has a 2.5mm bit. The smaller iron is ideal for electronic printed circuit board work, while the 25-watt is the general-purpose iron.

To make a good-quality soldered joint, heat the iron for at least 5 minutes. Don't rush this heating-up time as the iron's tip must be up to full temperature. Have to hand a damp, soldering iron tip-cleaning sponge or pad. If you own a soldering iron stand, it is likely it came with a cleaning sponge; if not, cut a piece of ordinary sponge and use that. I have used pieces of old car-wash sponge, and best of all is a piece of cut-up kitchen cleaning sponge! Remember to keep the sponge damp.

Once the iron is hot, wipe the tip on the sponge to remove all previous oxidisation and any old solder residue. Assuming the tip is in good condition, apply a little of the rosin-cored solder to wet the tip. Never use solid stick-type solder with so called 'tinman's' flux, nor the paste or liquid types of flux, unless you want to completely ruin the electrical joint. Solid solder is only for use with solid sheet metals – loco building, plumbing, etc – while most liquid or paste fluxes have a considerable amount of acid in their mixture, which over a period of time will cause corrosion of the soldered electrical joint.

Before soldering a joint it must be completely grease-free and clean; ideally use a glass-fibre pen or scrape both surfaces of the items to be soldered with a knife blade to clean them, then, if both items are wires, twist-join them together. The only exception to the cleaning is where a freshly stripped wire is being soldered and the wire's sheathing has kept the wire's surface nice and clean. With the iron's tip coated in liquid solder (wetted), place the tip directly onto the connection. Wait a few seconds for the heat of the tip to transfer into the components, then apply a little cored solder to the heated joint, not to the iron's tip. You should see the solder start to melt and flow into and around the joint. Once sufficient solder has been applied to coat the whole joint, remove both iron and solder. Now

do not touch or move the joint. Wait for at least 10 seconds after removing the heat to allow the joint to cool and the solder to set. What you should end up with is a solid, clean joint. Where wires are soldered together, trim off any excess wire.

Sometimes the PVC sheath on the wire being soldered will shrink back a little. This is a nuisance at times and is due to the sheathing having a low temperature range or too much heat having been applied to the joint for too long.

Use heat-shrinkable tubing over any 'in-line' or other exposed joints; while it is a little more expensive than insulating tape, once shrunk down it gives a joint a more professional and secure finish. At times the use of PVC insulating tape cannot be avoided, as where a T-shaped spur occurs, eg where a wire is connected to a through wire.

Finally, before you go on to solder another joint, or when you have finished soldering and before you disconnect the iron, clean the tip again on the damp sponge. You will get many years of use from a soldering iron if you keep its tip clean! Never be tempted to take a file to a modern soldering iron's tip to try and return it to service. Most modern iron tips have a special coating applied, which the file will remove and the tip will not perform anywhere near as well as previously. Replacement tips are sold for most irons and normally only cost a fraction of the replacement cost of a complete iron. However, if no replacement part is available, purchasing a new iron is the answer.

The one thing the novice solderer should do is to practise and practise. Complete 20 or more trial solder joints and your skill will improve.

Track feeds

Track feed wires can be connected to a solid 'dropper', which has been soldered to the rail's outer face then passed down through a predrilled hole in the baseboard's surface, or the actual feed wire can be soldered directly to the rail's outer face, or its underside if the track has not already been laid, thus making it virtually invisible.

For solid wire droppers the track feed wiring insulation is stripped back by approximately 15mm; if there is a second wire going elsewhere,

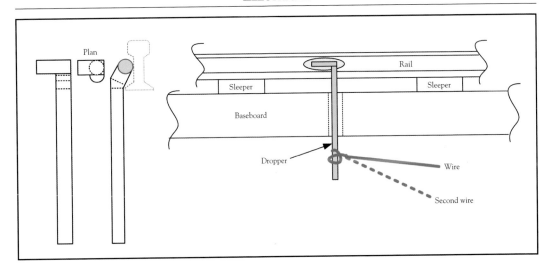

Above Figure 35: Solid dropper wires can be made from 1.0mm^2 non-insulated copper wire – a cheap source is the earth wire of a mains electric cable. The dropper wire is cut to approximately 1½ inches (40mm) long. One end is bent over at 90 degrees, then, just at the 90-degree bend, it is bent inwards at approximately 45 degrees to fit into the rail's web. Trim off the end of the bent section that will be soldered to the rail to a length of around 1/16 to 1/8 inch (1-2mm).

Right Track feed droppers passing through the baseboard and ready to be soldered in place.

Right The droppers soldered to the rail sides.

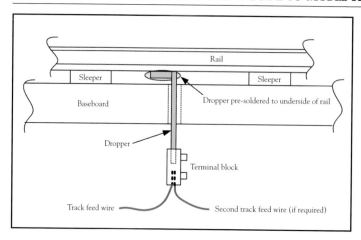

Figure 36: For those who find soldering underneath the railway baseboard difficult, a terminal block can be used on the end of the solid copper dropper.

that too is similarly stripped and twisted onto the first. The wire(s) are then twisted one and half turns around the dropper wire, which leaves a little excess wire protruding. Push the wire(s) up the dropper until they are about 1mm from the baseboard's underside. Solder the joint and, once cooled, cut off the surplus dropper wire and any surplus flexible wire not soldered onto the dropper (see Figures 35 and 36). Write in pencil on the board's underside next to the dropper the unique number of that

particular feed for future reference, and also record it in the wiring book.

Carry on running in all the track feed wires until they are all installed. This may well include some 'through feed' wires, which are not actually connected to the track on that particular baseboard, but feed other sections of track further round the layout. Remember to keep recording each wire in the diagram book!

I do not recommend using rail joiners (fishplates) as a place for soldering electrical rail

Figure 37: The problem of high resistance inside a rail joint can be overcome by having two track feeds close together, although in practice they could be 4-5 feet (1200-1550mm) apart, if for example the rails were full-length 36-inch (915mm) sections of flexible track.

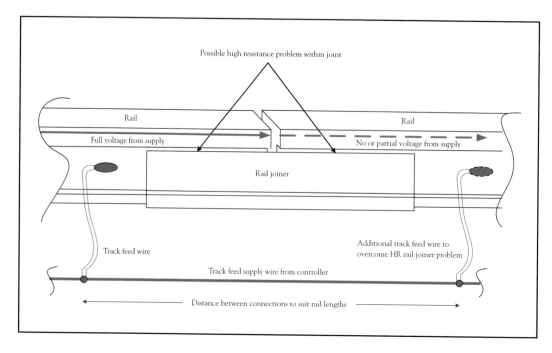

feeds. The reason for this is that the two abutting rails will be continually moving a little inside the joiner as they expand and contract, and this movement will ultimately introduce a high resistance (HR) into the joint on one or both sides of the joiner. This is caused by the small movement loosening the joiner, and microscopic dust particles in the air combining and making an almost invisible insulation between the two surfaces. Even paint, if the rails are painted a rust colour, can get inside the joiner and form an HR joint! This HR insulation prevents or severely restricts the flow of electrical current from the joiner to the rails. An affected rail joiner will often manifest itself by locomotives running erratically or stopping for no apparent reason on a certain piece of track. Thus it is far better to solder feed wires onto the rails themselves, even if this means installing several wires series-connected ('daisy chain' fashion) along the length of track being fed by that supply. Linking or bonding out of the joiners is another option, by using a small flexible wire soldered onto the outside of the rail web and running from rail to rail to bridge the joint – but I feel that these are more unsightly than the dropper wire (see Figure 37).

Switches

Switches come in various styles and many can be used as part of model railway electrical controls. Perhaps the most common switch is the 'toggle' switch, often the smaller 'miniature' style. The rotary switch is also popular, as this allows the making and breaking of many switching contacts with the turn of a central shaft and knob.

Switch terminology
Poles are the number of independent electrical parts within a single switch's body. A switch can have one or more poles; for example, 'SP' means Single Pole – one electrical input and output, while 'DP' is Double Pole – two independent and isolated electrical parts within the switch. 'TP' is therefore Triple Pole, or three independent and isolated parts within the switch's body.

Ways are the number of electrical paths or outlets a switch has. Thus a one-way switch is just a single on-off function connecting the input (common) tag to the output tag or

disconnecting the output tag when the lever is in the opposite position. A three-way switch would have three separate outputs from one common terminal, ie the switch can be moved to any of three positions and each position connects that outlet with the common terminal.

Throw is similar to 'way', and is the number of electrical outlets connected to the common tag. A Single Throw (ST) switch will only provide on-off switching, therefore the switch would only have two connection tags. A conventional house light switch is a 1-way Single Pole (SPST) switch. A Double Throw (DT) will make contact to either side of the switch dependant upon the toggle's or lever's position, ie a DT switch will provide on-on to the common tag. It will have three terminals or tags and is sometimes called a 'two-way switch' (just to confuse matters!). In all cases I have used the term C/O as meaning 'change over' when referring to switches. So, to reiterate, a DPDT configuration is two independent and separate electrical paths through a switch, and the switch's moving common contact travels from one contact set to the opposite contact set for both paths.

'Passing contact' switches
Some model railway manufactures, including Hornby and Peco, also supply signal box lever-style switches, which are often colour-coded to allow easy identification of their use. Hornby's R044 black point lever is a passing-contact type, providing off-(on)-(off)-(on)-off contact with the lever's wiring from one side to the other. Note that the bracketed positions are contact or non-contact positions, but are not capable of maintaining that position permanently due to the lever's full movement; similarly in the case of toggle switches, an internal spring returns the lever to another 'at rest' position. The Hornby R044 point lever is at rest at one end of the switch and not making contact – off. Then, as it is slowly moved over, it makes a contact (on), breaks that contact again in the middle position (off), makes contact with another position (on) and finally reaches the fully over position where it is off. This is called a 'passing contact' lever, as it passes two separate connection places in its travel (see Figure 38).

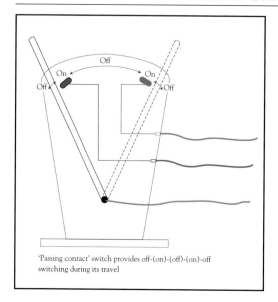

'Passing contact' switch provides off-(on)-(off)-(on)-off switching during its travel

Left Figure 38: An internal view of the Hornby R044 black 'passing contact' point lever switch. The lever carries the input current from the brown input connection, and as it is moved from rest it passes by the first (green) 'on' contact. If the point motor is already in that position the appropriate coil will still receive a pulse of current but will not move. No electrical contact is available in the central part of the lever's travel, then as it reaches the opposite end of its travel it makes contact with the opposite (red) contact. The point motor's other coil now receives a pulse of current while the lever is maintained in the red area. Finally the lever reaches fully over, the red connection is broken and the lever is at rest.

Below Three Hornby lever switches: the black R044 'passing contact' point switch, the yellow R046 lever switch with on-on contacts – ideal for switching two-aspect colour light signals, etc, and the green R047 lever offering on-off switching – ideal for track feed isolating sections or controlling building lighting. *Courtesy of and © copyright Hornby Hobbies Ltd*

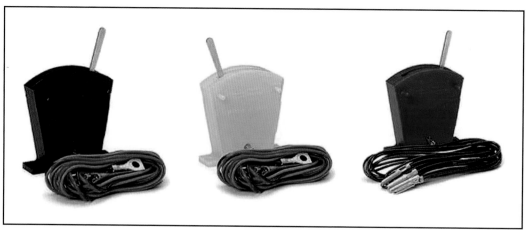

Below A typical miniature toggle switch of the Single Pole Double Throw (SPDT) type, which has three connections that can be wired. It provides an on-on option, as the central common tag is always in contact with one of the two outer tags and is controlled by the position of the toggle lever. This switch has been wired to operate a two-aspect colour light signal. The central (orange-wired) tag is the 12-volt dc input feed, and the two outer red and green tags carry the current away to the signal itself and provide the power to illuminate the selected aspect's lamp.

Below This toggle switch is a Double Pole Double Throw (DPDT) type. The switch now has an additional row of three contact tags, making six in all. The second row of three is electrically separate from the first row. This switch offers on-on switching by two separate poles or paths.

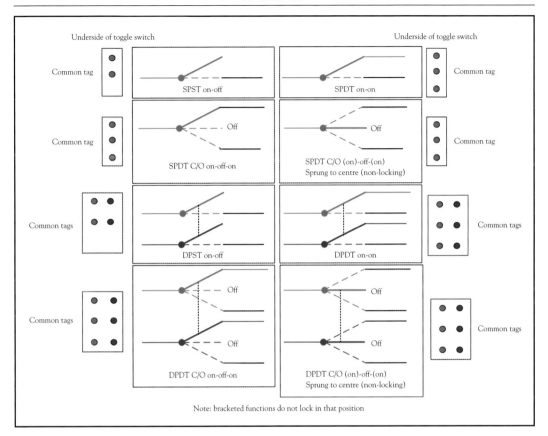

Underside of toggle switch

Common tag — SPST on-off

SPDT on-on — Common tag

Common tag — SPDT C/O on-off-on — Off

SPDT C/O (on)-off-(on)
Sprung to centre (non-locking) — Off — Common tag

Common tags — DPST on-off

DPDT on-on — Common tags

Common tags — DPDT C/O on-off-on — Off — Off

DPDT C/O (on)-off-(on)
Sprung to centre (non-locking) — Off — Off — Common tags

Note: bracketed functions do not lock in that position

Above Figure 39: Some toggle switch contact arrangements

Right This is a Double Pole Double Throw Centre Off (DPDT C/O) switch, which is spring-loaded (or biased) to the central off position. It looks similar to the DPDT switch, except that the toggle lever is held centrally by the internal spring and the toggle cannot lock over permanently in either of the two on positions. This type of switch, or its Single Pole equivalent, is ideal for operating a solenoid point motor where only a momentary pulse of power is required to operate it. The switch offers (on)-off-(on) selection, the bracketed positions indicating that the switch cannot remain there.

Yellow and green levers are also available from the same Hornby range. The yellow R046 lever provides on-on switching and is used for circuits that require two permanent feeds such as a two-aspect colour light. The green R047 provides on-off switching, and can be used for isolating track sections or turning any power feeds on and off.

Toggle switches

These are readily available in various contact formats and lever or toggle positions, ie on-off,

on-on, on-off-on, and on-off-on centre off, with some available as spring-loaded to the centre off position (on)-off-(on), or even some that are biased to one position, eg (on)-off or (off)-on, depending on exactly how they are wired. Remember that the switch cannot normally remain locked in the bracketed position.

Toggle switches, often in the miniature style, are favoured by many railway modellers over the lever type of switch. The toggle switch is often mounted in a small panel, or even a 'mimic panel' (of which more later). Many varieties of switch contact and lever position are available in the toggle switch range, so the buyer needs to be fully aware of the exact type needed for a particular use. Figure 39 shows a few of the toggle switch contact arrangements most commonly found for model railway use.

Slide switches

The use of slide switches in model railway electrical wiring is quite common, and these can be used for switching on or off isolating sections and special track feeds, or operating accessories that require an on-on power arrangement, such as electrically lit colour light signals. They are, however, not suitable for powering solenoid point motors as their contacts remain closed continually while the slide lever is in either position.

A Double Pole Double Throw (DPDT) slide switch.

Rotary switches

These offer many contacts and normally several positions, or clicks, of the rotary shaft (or knob, when fitted). Typically these can be 4-pole 3-way to 1-pole 12-way. Don't get confused here: 'ways' are the number of positions to which a rotary switch can be turned, eg a 3-way rotary switch can be turned to any of three positions, while the 12-way can turn to any of 12 positions. So for example a 12-way 1-pole rotary switch can click or turn to 12 positions, but it only has one input (way) physically connected to any one of the 12 output positions. However, a 4-pole 3-way switch can turn to any of three positions and it

has four inputs (poles) that can give any of three outputs each! (See Figure 40.) To confuse matters still more, rotary switches can be supplied in 'Make before Break' or 'Break before Make' configurations! For model railway use the 'Break before Make' style is the one normally needed, as we need to ensure that the circuit being switched is disconnected before the next circuit is connected.

A 4-pole 3-way rotary switch. The four central tags (poles) are the common connections and are connected to their respective outer tags (ways), in this case one of three, depending on the rotary shaft's position.

Cab control

Cab control is a means of switching one or more sections of track between two or more controllers. It allows each controller, when the appropriate selection switch has been operated, to operate in full the track power over that section of line.

A typical example may be a station goods yard, which is switched between possibly two or three controllers; for example, Controller 1 normally operates the up main line and Controller 2 the down main line, while Controller 3, if available, is used to work either up or down lines and also the goods yard. By arranging the selection switching further, any of

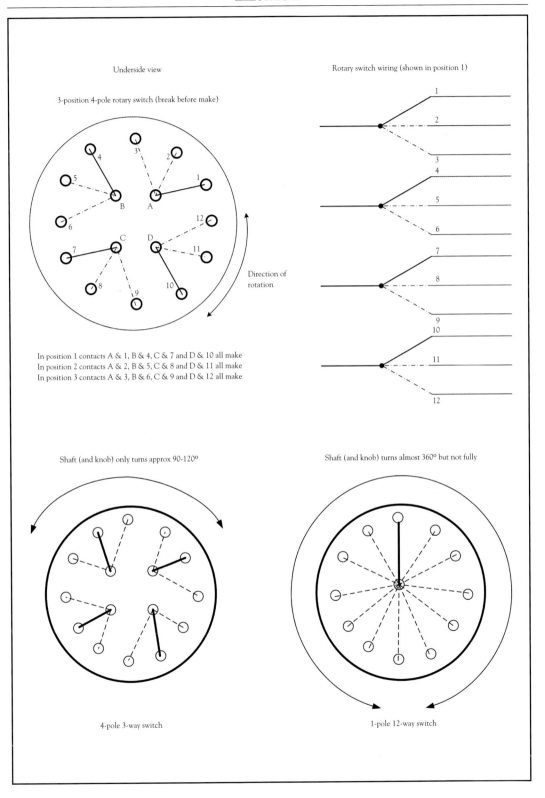

Underside view

Rotary switch wiring (shown in position 1)

3-position 4-pole rotary switch (break before make)

Direction of rotation

In position 1 contacts A & 1, B & 4, C & 7 and D & 10 all make
In position 2 contacts A & 2, B & 5, C & 8 and D & 11 all make
In position 3 contacts A & 3, B & 6, C & 9 and D & 12 all make

Shaft (and knob) only turns approx 90-120°

Shaft (and knob) turns almost 360° but not fully

4-pole 3-way switch

1-pole 12-way switch

Figure 40: Rotary switch configurations

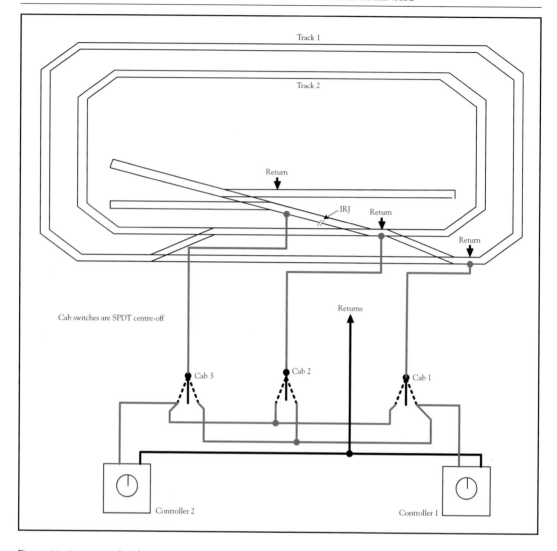

Figure 41: A very simple cab control system. 'Cab 1' and 'Cab 2' can be switched to either circuit of track (Track 1 and Track 2), while 'Cab 3' controls the sidings. Any 'Cab' can be connected to either controller. In reality, the track sections would be divided up into many isolated sections by using IRJs and the 'Cabs' switched into each section as needed.

the controllers could be switched to operate each other's sections. In the example in Figure 41, once the appropriate points are moved,

Controller 1 could drive a train from the up main line (outer track) to the down line (inner track), then right into the goods yard.

7
POINTS

Live and dead frogs

There are basically two types of model railway points – those with live frogs (sometimes termed Electrofrog) and those with insulated or dead frogs (Insulfrog). The two types are very similar in appearance except the dead-frog type has its frog manufactured from plastic, hence it is 'insulated'. The dead frog is the simplest to use and is often the choice of the newcomer, since it does not require any additional work other than installation in the correct position on the layout; it switches track power from one direction to the other and leaves the direction for which it is not set electrically isolated or off (see Figure 42).

The live-frog point does offer better running than the dead-frog type, as there is no insulated area where a small-wheeled loco might lose power. The live frog provides optimum slow-running performance as a loco travels over the point slowly. The small down-side of this improvement is the need to fit two insulated rail joiners (IRJs) after the frog, normally on the ends of the two vee rails leading away from the frog, as these two rails swap polarity as the point moves over and back; without the IRJs a short circuit would occur (see Figure 43). There are other options that the user of live-frog points can employ to achieve even better running: frog polarity switching (see page 89) and bonding the switch rail to its adjacent stock rail once insulations are fitted into both closure rails.

Sets of points on the author's layout.

Mechanical point operation

The next choice is how we want to make the point blades move, and there are several options open to the modeller. The simplest is the 'finger method', where the operator's finger appears on the layout and pushes the point's tie bar over and back as required. This is fine so long as you can reach all the points!

Perhaps the first of the remote control operating methods is the 'wire in tube' system, which uses a flexible wire inside a flexible tube,

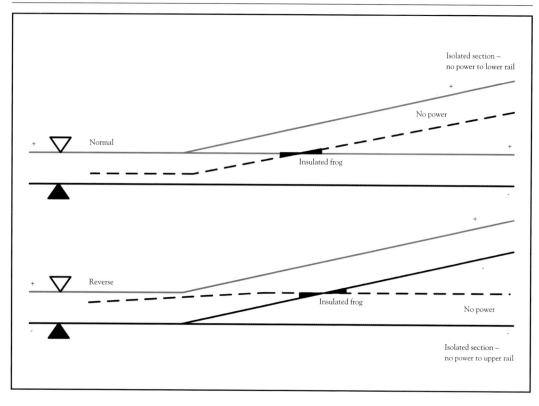

Above Figure 42: How an insulated-frog (Insulfrog) point switches the track power dependant upon its position

Below Figure 43: Point switching with a live frog (Electrofrog)

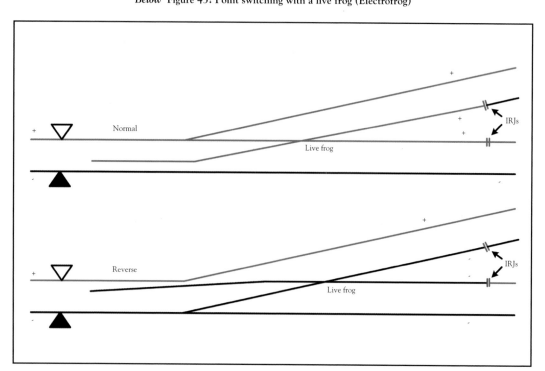

Above A Peco code 100 insulated-frog (Insulfrog) point. Note the all-plastic frog or crossing tip.

Below A Peco code 100 live-frog (Electrofrog) point. Note here that the frog or crossing is all-metal.

much like a bicycle brake system. One end of the wire is connected to the point's tie bar while the other end appears some distance away at the side of the baseboard, often with a small push-pull knob. The tubing in which the wire moves is held in place by small clips or staples on the underside of the baseboard.

Point rodding and mechanical levers is another method, employing a similar technique to that used on the real railway before electrically operated points were used. Solid rodding is moved back and forth by a lever, with right-angle cranks transferring the push or pull movement through right-angles. Electric solenoid coil motors or small electric motors can be used to drive a little gear train to drive the point blades over and back.

Electrical point operation

Electrically operated points are often the chosen method, and the next items to consider are how these will operate and their wiring requirements. Two types are common, the solenoid motor (technically not a 'motor' in the true sense) and the electric point motor, often called a 'stall motor'.

To ensure reliable operation of the solenoid motor, a Capacitor Discharge Unit (CDU) is recommended; just one is normally required for the whole layout. The CDU provides a momentary pulse of high power to the solenoid's coil via the selection switch, thereby overcoming any slight stiffness within the point motor or the point itself. It is wired directly across the 16- to 24-volt point supply transformer's output. Consider the use of a 24-volt ac supply for solenoid point operation together with a CDU, as this provides that little extra power often needed where several motors are to be moved simultaneously. However, there is no reason why a 16-volt ac supply could not feed the point motors equally as well. Using a CDU reduces the current drawn from the transformer and also protects the solenoid coil, or motor as they are often referred to, from any possible continuous powering, which leads eventually to coil burn-out. I always advocate investing in a CDU – they actually cost little more than two new motors!

Point motors (solenoids) can be operated by several methods – 'passing contact' lever switches, toggle switches with a centre off position, stud and probe, or push buttons. In each case the use of a CDU will ensure reliable operation. You will of course need to operate more than one point on a layout, and all that is required is more studs or switches, together with the necessary wiring (two wires per motor plus return).

Touching the relevant stud with the probe or

moving the switch over allows the CDU to fire a 'one-shot' discharge current through the appropriate stud or switch contact and out via the wiring to the motor's coil winding. However, only 'passing contact' or spring-loaded centre-off switches must be used, otherwise where a CDU is not being used the motor's coil will receive full power continuously and quickly burn out. When two or more sets of points are required to be operated at once, as in the case of a crossover, simply wire the first motor to the second, ensuring that the electrical path for the 'normal' direction is correctly orientated on both points and that the same coils are wired together. Most CDUs can operate up to three motors simultaneously, and those sold as 'heavy duty' often can throw up to six motors at once.

Route setting by the use of a diode matrix is another option for point control, but remember that each diode looses 0.7v in volt drop! Thus

Below Figure 44: Basic wiring for a typical lever-operated solenoid point motor using a Hornby R044 black 'passing contact' lever. This is probably the simplest means of powering an electric point motor. Note the CDU in the feed circuit; this can if wished be omitted, with the two wires from the supply (brown and black) feeding directly to the switch and motor respectively. (It should be noted that while the wiring colours shown in this illustration are normally used, some pre-wired point motors may use different colours – always check the manufacture's wiring guide.)

your matrix's input voltage needs to be higher than perhaps the normal 16 volts often used. I prefer to 'route set' on the mimic control panel by actually following a route manually along its path and setting points as I pass each stud or switch.

The use of, for example, Tortoise or Fulgarex slow-acting motors is another option; these do not require probes and studs, but do need switches that keep the motor's power supply on all the time they are moving, and sometimes continuously. Here no CDU is needed, as the motors operate directly from a power supply, nominally 12 volts dc, and the operating switch does not need to be of the sprung-to-centre type.

Wiring for the different types of operations is shown in Figures 44-46.

Right Figure 45: Wiring for a very simple stud and probe switching method normally used on mimic panels. Blue has been used to show the motor operation wires, but they can be any colour.

Below right Figure 46: In this almost identical diagram a dedicated point switch (a centre-off toggle switch sprung to the centre) is used, but it could equally be a pair of push-to-make non-locking push buttons. Note that both Figure 45 and Figure 46 offer the choice of a 16- or 24-volt ac supply (24 volts is my preference). A CDU is shown in both but, if omitted, the wires from the PSU would continue directly to the probe or switch's common tab and the other output feed would go directly to all the motors' return connection.

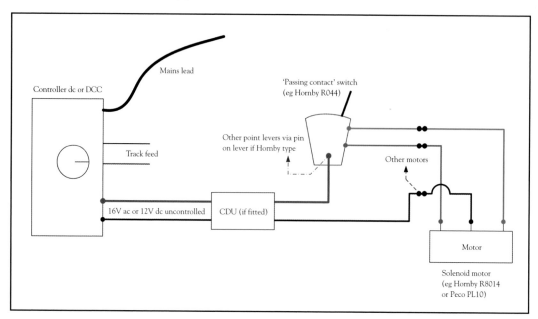

Controller dc or DCC

Mains lead

'Passing contact' switch
(eg Hornby R044)

Track feed

Other point levers via pin
on lever if Hornby type

Other motors

16V ac or 12V dc uncontrolled

CDU (if fitted)

Motor

Solenoid motor
(eg Hornby R8014
or Peco PL10)

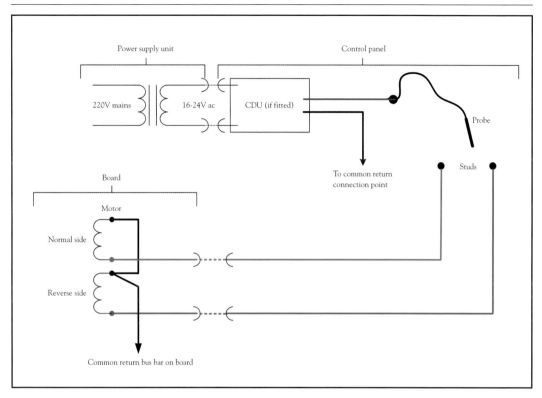

Power supply unit

Control panel

220V mains   16-24V ac   CDU (if fitted)

Probe

Studs

To common return
connection point

Board

Motor

Normal side

Reverse side

Common return bus bar on board

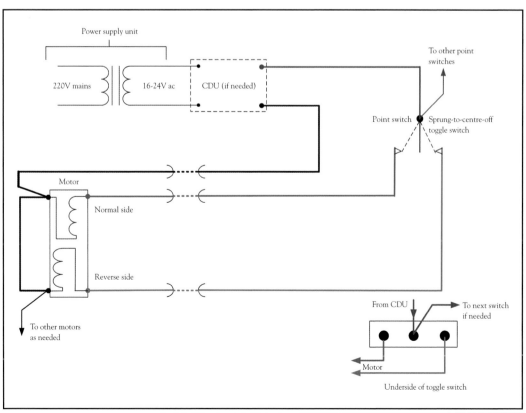

Power supply unit

To other point
switches

220V mains   16-24V ac   CDU (if needed)

Point switch   Sprung-to-centre-off
toggle switch

Motor

Normal side

Reverse side

To other motors
as needed

From CDU   To next switch
if needed

Motor

Underside of toggle switch

There is an alternative to the single-CDU method of point operation, and that is the 'single feed wire' point operation circuit. This removes the need for a common CDU for all point motors, but does involve having one capacitor and two diodes per motor; it also allows the use of a non-spring-loaded switch (see Figures 47 and 48). A SPDT (Single Pole Double Throw) switch can, if desired, be built into a mimic control panel or console; the advantage here is that, after throwing the point, the switch remains in that position, therefore its toggle or lever gives a visual indication of the position of the point on the layout. A 'passing contact' or centre-off switch is not required. Note that this circuit must be fed from a dc power source and have a 1000uf to 2200uf 35v minimum working electrolytic capacitor in series with the two 3-amp diodes. Failure to fit the capacitor will result in the motor being permanently connected to

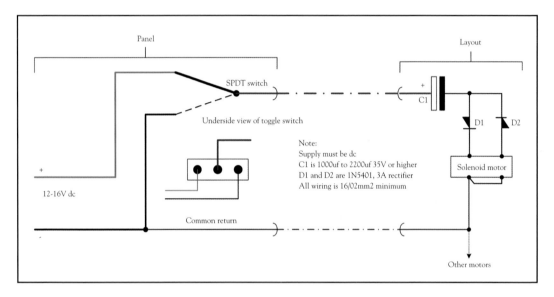

Above Figure 47: 'Single feed wire' point operation with individual capacitor

Below Figure 48: The actual layout of the components. They have been connected onto a four-way terminal strip, which is located as close as possible to the motor it is to operate.

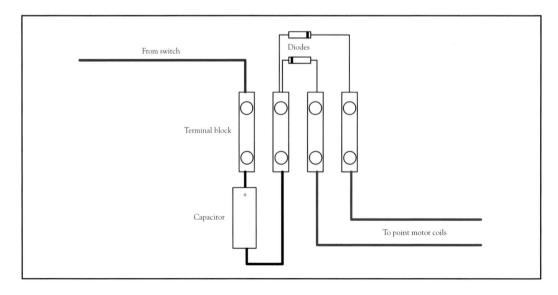

the supply and this will lead to rapid coil burn-out. Also ensure that the two diodes are fitted with opposite polarity to each other. The power supply *must* be dc and provide between 16 and 24 volts.

If the motor throws the opposite way from the switch's toggle position, reverse either the positive and negative connections on the switch, or swap over the diode wires where they connect to the motor coil terminals.

Be warned that electrolytic capacitors retain their charge for a long period of time after the power supply has been turned off. Never work on live capacitor circuits, and for those that have been previously live, always discharge the capacitor before working on the circuit.

Point motors

Point motors, or solenoids to be more specific, are two independent electrically operated coils that, when powered, produce a magnetic pull upon a central pin. The pin is pulled by induced magnetism across into the hollow central area of the coil that is being energised, which produces the movement needed to move the point's tie bar.

These motors are sometimes called 'snap action' point motors, from the noise they make as they operate over and back. To call them 'motors' is technically incorrect as there is no actual electric motor in a solenoid, although it has become the recognised term. However, actual electric-motor-driven point machines are available from manufactures such as Tortoise and Fulgarex. These operate in a slightly different method from the solenoid motor; some require a permanent dc feed to their drives, which if applied to a solenoid motor would quickly burn out the coil of the solenoid, rendering the motor useless.

Figure 49 shows the wiring required for a Peco PL10 point motor. This motor can also have a PL13 or PL15 twin accessory switch fitted to it, which will provide point-operated switching functions (see Figure 50). The PL10 is sold in three versions. PL10 is the basic motor with a shortened drive pin, which is normally a direct fitting onto the underside of a Peco point. The PL10E has an extended drive pin and is used where the motor is fixed underneath a baseboard;

the longer drive pin passes up through the baseboard and into the hole in the point tie bar. Finally the PL10W has a slightly higher coil resistance (approximately 10.4ohms) and is ideal for use with DCC accessory decoder outputs where a reduced operating current is needed. It has the short drive pin and is therefore ideal for direct mounting. A PL10WE is also available.

The Seep PM1 motor offers similar point control to that of the Peco motor. However, it also has a manufacturer-fitted change-over switch, and the switched normal and reverse contacts operated by the motor can be of great use to the modeller. They can be used, for example, on a mimic panel as indications of the actual position of the points, control signal aspects, or even illuminate junction indicators on colour light signals; where live-frog points are used they can also provide the track power switching to the frog.

Note in Figure 51 the six-way terminal strip block. This allows easy off-layout pre-wiring of the motor and the motor-operated switch, and provides a suitable place to connect incoming wires once the motor and block have been mounted on the layout; it also provides a test place. In all cases, terminals T1, T2 and T3 are all motor coil supplies, while T4, T5 and T6 are for point-operated switch contacts.

Frog polarity switching

This technique can be used on live-frog (Electrofrog) points – but *not* insulated-frog points. The point is wired to enable the best electrical connection through the point and to remove the need to rely solely on the electrical contact made between the switch blade and the fixed stock rail, which can prove troublesome at times. It also enhances slow running over the closed switch rail and on past the frog. A pair of change-over contacts are fitted to the point motor, and they swap the polarity of the frog as the point motor and its point blades move from one side to the other. So, in one position the frog is at a positive track supply voltage, then the point is moved over and the motor-operated switch flips the track power to the frog to a negative supply (see Figure 52, and Figure 43 earlier in this chapter).

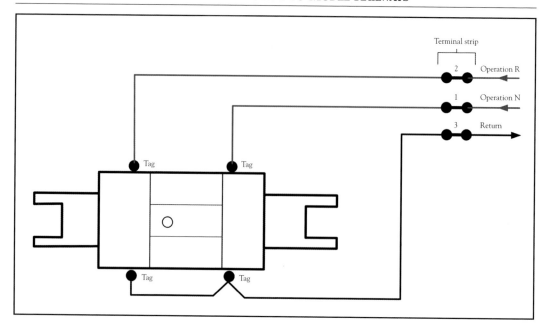

Above Figure 49: The wiring required for a Peco PL10 solenoid motor. Note the two coil tags that become the returns and are wired together with a wire link.

Left A Peco PL10E motor fitted with a PL13 accessory switch and mounted under the baseboard.

Below Figure 50: A Peco PL13 accessory switch and how its internal contact changes over the feed from the common tag to either of the two opposite end tags depending on which way the point motor has moved.

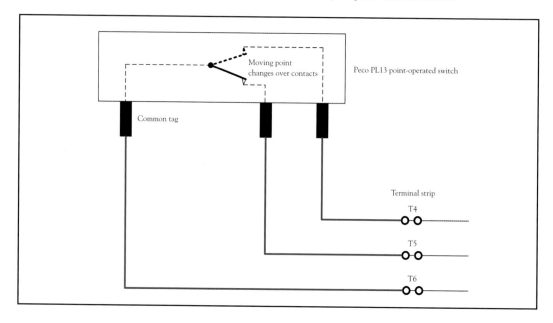

Right A Seep PM1 motor shown upside-down to provide a clearer view of the six solder connection pads – A to F – running along the edge of the motor.

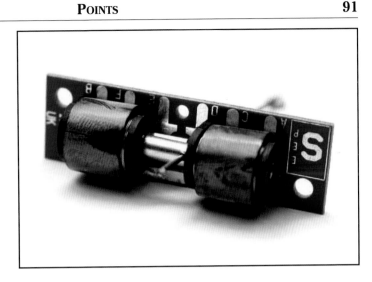

Below Figure 51: The coil and contact wiring for the Seep PM1 motor

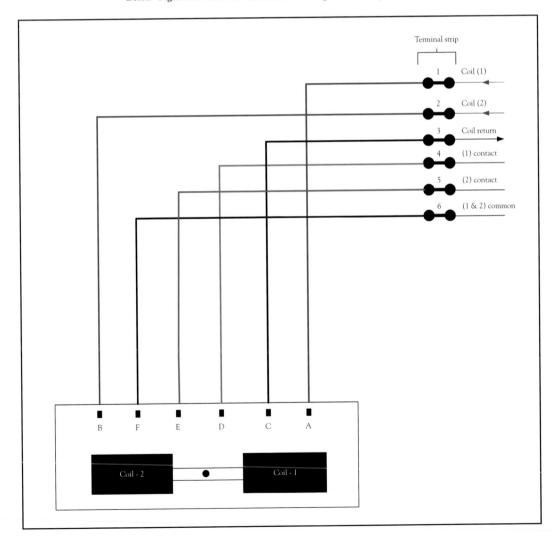

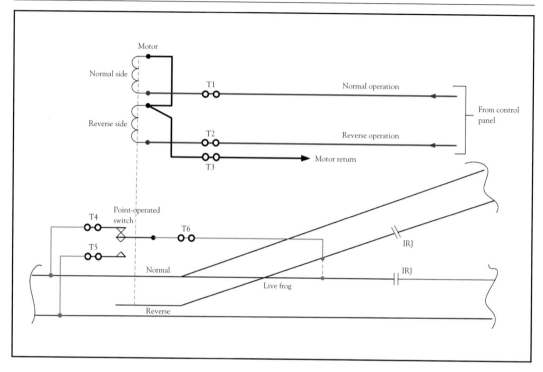

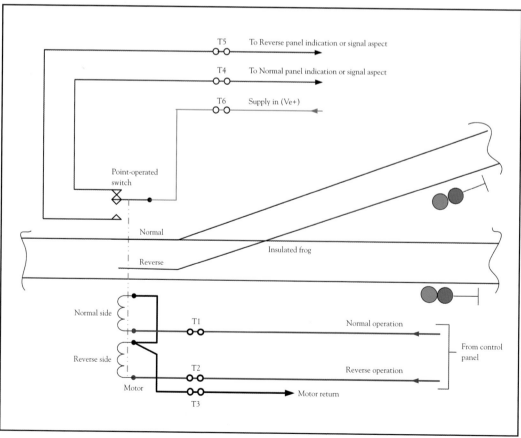

Left Figure 52: Live frog polarity switching. Note the need to fit the two insulated rail joiners (IRJs) after the frog on live-frog points.

Below left Figure 53: Basically the same layout, but using an insulated-frog point. Users of insulated-frog points can use the point-motor-operated switch for mimic panel point indications or to control colour light signal aspects.

Above A three-way point.

Below Figure 54: Wiring diagram for a three-way point. All the power is fed via a CDU to ensure that a sufficient pulse is sent to the two motors. Additionally, and to ensure that only the correct motor coils operate, a four-diode matrix is wired between the switch's outputs and the actual motor coils.

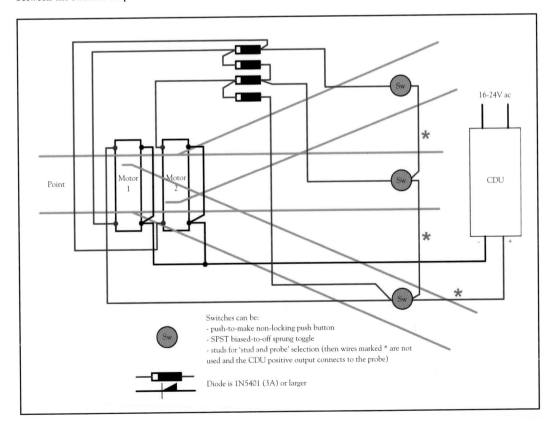

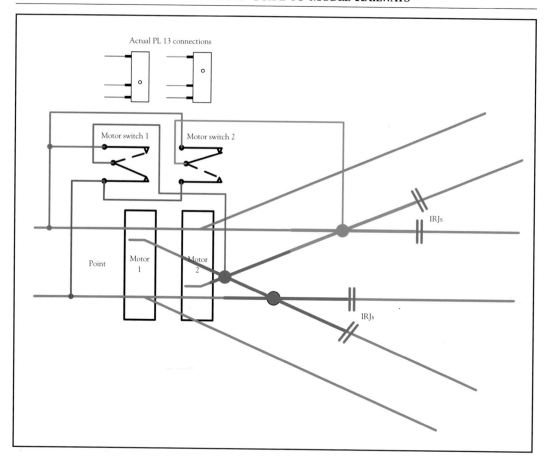

Above Figure 55: Wiring a live-frog three-way point. Factory-installed insulated rail joints within the pointwork have been omitted for clarity.

Below A Peco code 100 double slip with insulated (dead) frogs. These are much easer to wire than their live Electrofrog counterparts.

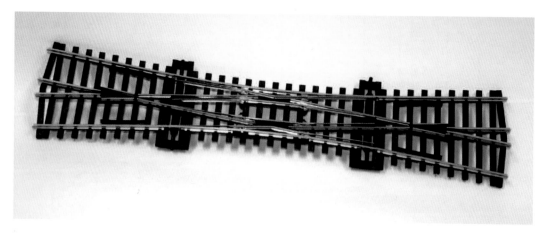

Above right Figure 56: Wiring for a live-frog (Electrofrog) double slip (dc or DCC)

Right Figure 57: The Peco double slip is wired as in Figure 56, but this diagram shows the additional factory-fitted wires.

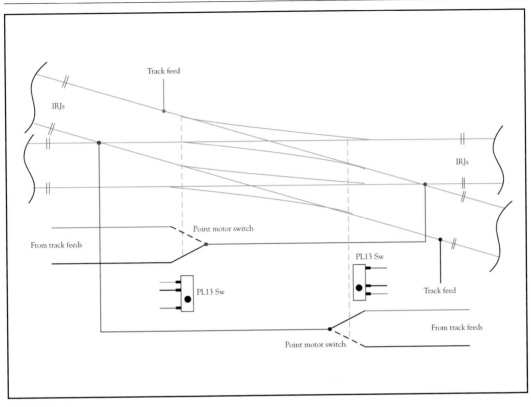

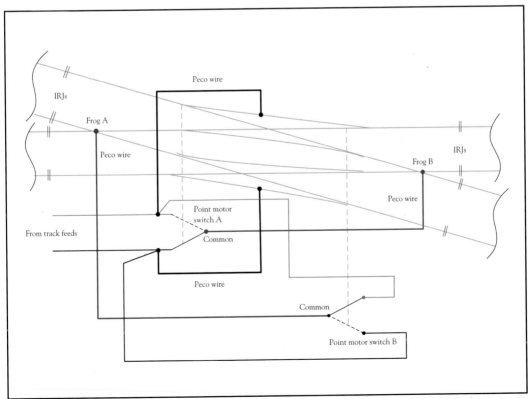

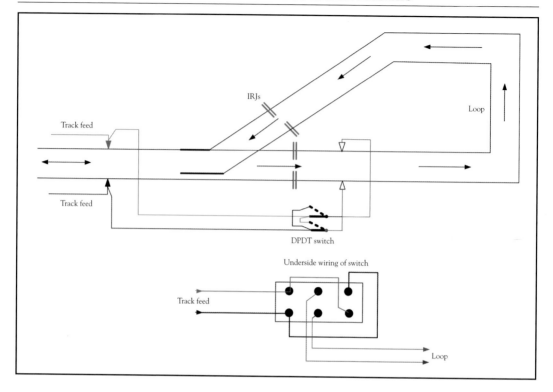

Above Figure 58: Wiring a reversing loop with a DPDT switch. The underside wiring detail of the toggle switch is shown in the smaller drawing.

Below Figure 59: Wiring the reversing loop points using a 4-pole relay

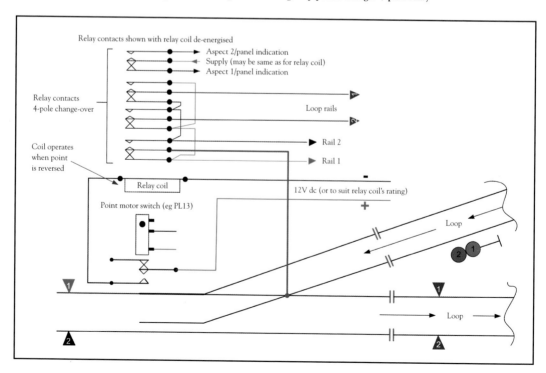

Three-way point operation sometimes causes concern, but with an insulated-frog type it is really quite simple, and Figure 54 shows a circuit using three push-to-make momentary-push buttons, although these could quite easily be replaced by sprung (biased) toggle switches or studs if using the stud and probe method of operation.

Frog polarity switching on a three-way live-frog (Electrofrog) point is a little more complex. The two point motors each have point switches fitted and they are wired as shown in Figure 55.

Double slip points, especially live-frog examples and their wiring, are another item that often causes problems for the newcomer. It really isn't too difficult, and if the two ends of the slip are considered to be no more than two normal single-ended points placed together, the wiring is quite straightforward (see Figure 56). If you have a Peco fine-scale Electrofrog double slip, it will already have four wires factory-fitted, and these connect to the two frogs and to the two outer rails (see Figure 57).

Reversing loops

Reversing loops need special wiring, using a DPDT switch as a means of reversing the loop's rail polarity. This is necessary because when a train enters the loop it must have the track polarity of the loop reversed before it can exit the loop and proceed back along the track it approached on. This is easily undertaken by installing four insulated rail joints, two at each end of the loop just after the loop points, and wiring in a Double Pole Double Throw (DPDT) switch. Note that the length of the switched loop section must be greater than the longest power unit to be run into it – ideally the section should be the full length of the loop.

The method of operation is as follows. The loop point and DPDT switch are set for an incoming train, and the train fully enters the loop's insulated section. The controller's power is then turned off, the point is changed and the DPDT switch is reversed. The controller's direction switch is changed to the opposite direction of travel and the power turned back on; the train will now leave the loop correctly (see Figure 58).

For those who wish to undertake it, automated loop switching can be used. Here a DPDT change-over switch can be fitted to the loop's controlling point; for example, a Peco PL15 twin micro-switch could replace the toggle switch. When the point moves over to allow the train already in the loop to leave, the loop's track polarity is swapped automatically. Similarly, a four-pole change-over relay could be used, so that if a live-frog point is being used frog-switching could be achieved via one set of relay contacts and the loop's rail polarity switched via two other sets of contacts. The fourth set of change-over contacts could be used for point indications or to control a signal aspect (see Figure 59).

8
CONTROL PANELS, INDICATIONS AND LIGHTING

Mimic panels

Mimic panels are miniature replicas of the whole or part of the track plan of the actual layout, and are sometimes used by the 'signaller' to set routes and operate signals, as per the real thing. The panel will have the track plan shown as a solid line representing each track – car lining tape is ideal for this. Points and signal control via panel-mounted switches will all be operated from here; real-time indications can be sent back to the panel to show point positions, while signal aspect indications can also be displayed.

The panel's surface can be made from any suitable material such as white-faced hardboard, MDF, Perspex or sheet metal such as aluminium. The body of the panel is often made from MDF or ply. Some panels are not mounted on boxes, but are simply a flat or upright facia fitted onto the baseboard.

Figure 60 shows a boxed mimic panel. The box could be free-standing and placed on a suitable table adjacent to the layout, or could be suspended from the layout's timber bracing by means of slide-together 'secret' fixing plates; one half of the plate is fitted to the layout and the mating half to the rear of the panel, and two or three sets of fixings will be needed for a medium-sized panel. Electrical connections transferring the circuits between panel and layout are often made via 'sub D' multi-pin connectors and either multi-core cables or individual flexible wires made up into multi-way bunches. Using 'sub D' connectors or other multi-pin plugs and sockets enables the panel to be removed and stored easily.

Mimic panels can also include the train speed controllers, in which case it is normal to use the specially manufactured panel-mounting versions. Additionally, hand-held controllers are often used, being plugged into the panel by means of multi-pin plugs and sockets such as the DIN 4 or 5 pin type.

Route indications on a control panel, which illuminate to show the direction in which the points are set and the selected path or route of the approaching train, can be easily made with LEDs (see below). These can be wired by using the 12-volt uncontrolled output of a controller or via a separate transformer, whose output is passed via a bridge rectifier to convert the ac into dc. The output then feeds all the point-motor-mounted switches, which in turn illuminate the point/route-setting indication LEDs on the panel's fascia.

There are two versions. The first uses two wires from the point-operated switch back to the panel and employs just one common positive 12-volt feed wire, which is run around the layout. Onto this common positive wire is connected a wire going to every point switch's 'common' tag for every point motor switch. Two wires then feed back to the panel and, via resistors, feed the appropriate route's LED(s). The arrangement is shown in Figure 61.

Where a larger number of point indications need to be returned to the mimic panel, another method of wiring uses just one wire per point end back to the panel. Again, the 12-volt dc uncontrolled controller's output is used or, if preferred, a special power supply providing 12 volts dc can be provided. The outputs of the supply (12-volt positive and 12-volt negative) are both run in a 'bus' format around the layout. Two wires, which connect one to each bus, are taken to the point-operated switches change-over wiring connections. From the point motor switch's 'common' tag there is just one wire per point end back to the panel (saving considerable

Figure 60: The construction of a typical mimic panel

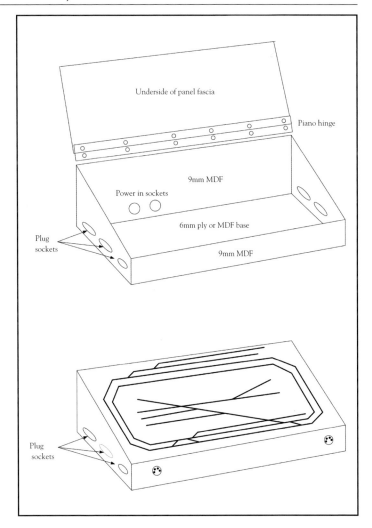

A hand-held controller fitted with a DIN 5 five-pin plug – only four pins of the plug are actually wired. A mating five-way chassis socket is fitted into the panel, connecting the controller to its power supply and taking the two track feed wires to the rails it controls.

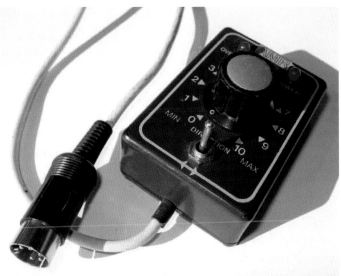

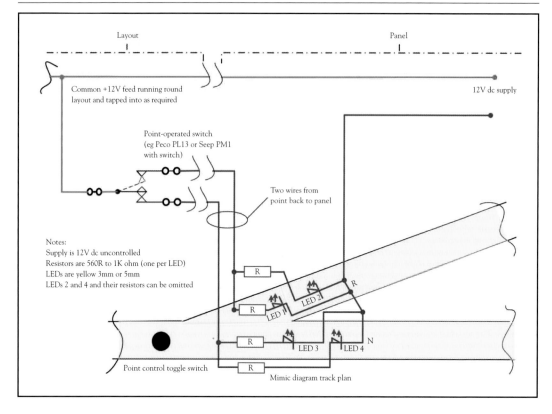

Figure 61: Using point-operated switches to illuminate route-indicating LEDs

wiring on a larger layout!), and this illuminates the appropriate group of LEDs, which may be a line of two or three made up from, ideally, 3mm yellow LEDs. In addition, this 12-volt supply 'bus' can be used to power other accessories such as signal lamps and any building or street-scene illumination.

Two or three LEDs are mounted in the mimic panel's track diagram per route direction and all are fed via individual resistors, one per LED. It is important to note that in the single-wire circuit, one route's direction LEDs are wired opposite from that of the other route, ie when the point-activated switch is moved from normal to reverse the polarity being fed to that route's LEDs along the single wire is changed over, so it is necessary to ensure that the 'reverse' route's LEDs are wired the opposite way from the 'normal' set route (see Figure 62).

Where a route includes a crossover, from, say, the up line to the down line, four LEDs illuminate that route, ie two per point end.

The 12-volt dc lighting power 'bus' starts at the mimic panel, then goes out onto the layout to feed the individual point-motor-fitted switches. Use a suitable size of wire for this lighting 'bus' to prevent serious volt drop and to ensure that the full current available from the power supply is also available on the layout. Typically this can be either 16/0.2mm^2 or 24/0.2mm^2 wire.

Point switches

Point switches on the mimic panel are normally of the toggle type, and are mounted directly into the plan on the panel's fascia. Usually, SPDT sprung-to-centre-off switches are used to operate points. However, SPDT conventional on-on toggle switches can be used under certain circumstances, as detailed previously in Chapter 7 when describing 'single wire and return' operation. Some panels may use stud and probe point selection instead of switches, while others may use push-to-make non-locking push-buttons, where two push-buttons are used per point.

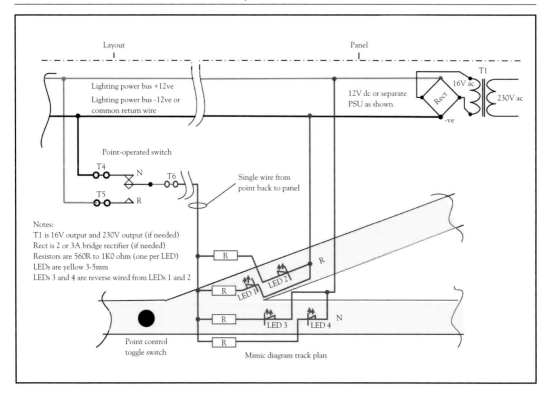

Figure 62: Wiring diagram for a simplified single-lead point-end route indication on a mimic panel

Signal switches

Signal switches on the mimic panel are often toggle or rotary switches, mounted to the side of the track plan. Rotary switches offer the multi-aspect-signal user the availability to control all the signal's aspects individually. Normally signal indications display only a red or green indication light via a bi-coloured LED mounted adjacent to the switch. It is not really necessary to show all the colours of the proceed aspects of the signal – only a green 'OFF' indication need be displayed. Of course, for a signal that does not show a stop (red) aspect, such as a Distant signal, the red/green should be replaced with a yellow/green bi-coloured LED.

LEDs and lamps

LEDs (Light Emitting Diodes)

LEDs come in all sorts of colours, sizes and brightness, from the tiny 0.8mm to the huge 10mm or larger versions. They run virtually cold and last for many years, and all work on the same principle: apply the correct dc voltage and the

LED will light! It is applying the correct voltage and limiting the current available that often causes the newcomer so much trouble! In the main, to be at their brightest most basic 3mm- or 5mm-diameter LEDs require around 2.2 volts at around 20 milliamps of current. There are exceptions, but these figures apply to most normal LEDs. However, a check of the manufacture's data sheet will confirm the actual values.

How can the LEDs operate safely from our model railway power supply? Basically, a suitable series resistor is wired into the LED feed path or circuit, one resistor for each LED. Quite a simple formula is used to calculate the minimum acceptable value of resistance needed. Assume that the power supply is 12 volts dc. The forward voltage of a standard LED is around 2.2 volts, and its ideal forward current is around 20 milliamps, so the safe value minimum resistance formula is: 12v (the supply voltage) minus 2.2 (the forward LED volts) divided by 20 milliamps (the forward LED current). Thus 12 - 2.2 = 9.8, which, divided by 0.020, gives an answer of 490,

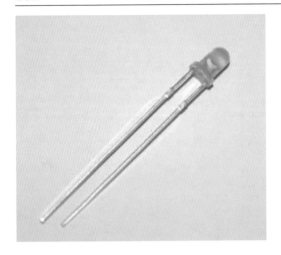

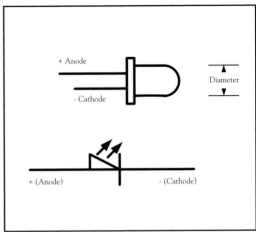

Above A typical yellow 3mm-diameter LED. The longer lead is the positive or Anode connection.

Above Figure 63: An LED, and how it is represented in a wiring diagram

Below Figure 64: The upper diagram shows one LED operating from a dc supply, while in the lower drawing the same LED is powered from an ac supply; note the inverse diode fitted across the LED's supply. The inverse diode can be any small diode such as a 1N4148 or 1N4001.

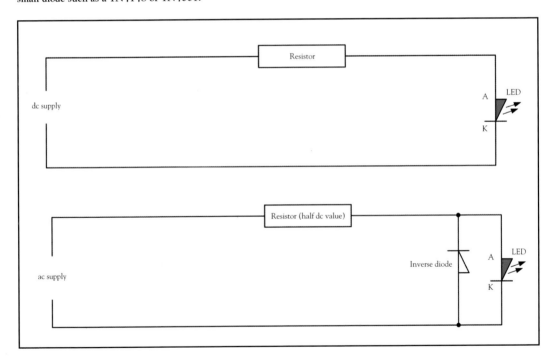

which is the exact value of the resistance needed.

Unfortunately, resistors are not available in this value! The nearest preferred value above the calculation is 510 or 560 ohms (510R or 560R). In most cases the resistor is rated at 0.25 watt, but a larger wattage can be chosen to run the LED if a quarter-watt isn't available. Higher-value ohm resistors can be used and these will, as the resistance value considerably increases, cause the LED to run less brightly. I have found that there is little difference in light output when using a 560R or 1K resistor, but after that a small reduction in brightness will be seen.

However, an LED is likely to last longer if the resistance value is a little higher than calculated.

It is vitally important to remember that LEDs are polarity-conscious devices, therefore when connected to a dc supply (with a suitable series resistance) they will only illuminate when the positive supply is connected to the correct LED wire (usually the longer lead of the two). If you want to run an LED on ac, an inverse diode should be wired across the LED, and the resistance value calculated in the formula given above is then halved (see Figure 64).

LEDs offer excellent illumination of buildings or street lights, station lamps, etc, and many can be operated from one power supply. Typically a 12-volt dc 1.0 amp supply could power 50 LEDs, though in practice a slightly smaller number should be connected to allow a little margin on the power supply. They are wired in parallel, and if all are to be turned on or off at the same time a Single Pole Single Throw (SPST) toggle switch or similar can be wired into the positive feed leg immediately after the power supply, as shown in Figure 65.

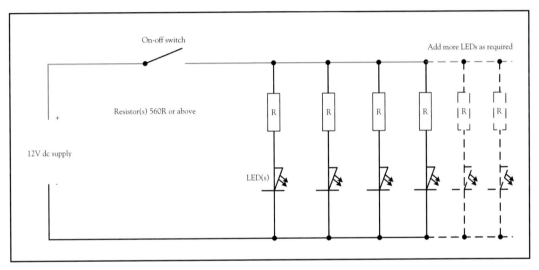

Above Figure 65: LEDs wired in parallel with an SPST toggle switch

Below Figure 66: The same arrangement as in Figure 65, but with a 16-volt ac supply and a bridge rectifier

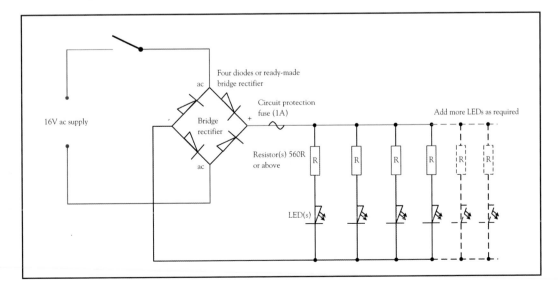

If a 16-volt ac power supply is used, a bridge rectifier is connected immediately after the supply to convert the ac into dc. The option of switching the whole circuit on and off is again controlled by an SPST switch. A suitable fuse can be inserted in either circuit to offer circuit protection (see Figure 66).

Filament lamps

'Grain of wheat' (GoW) or the smaller 'Grain of rice' (GoR) lamps are commonly used in model railways. While they both offer excellent illumination and are available in various colours,

unfortunately they have two downfalls: one is that they often tend to run extremely hot, and the other is that they can each draw a considerable amount of current from the power supply.

Whenever possible try and 'under run' these lamps to prolong their life. That is, if the lamp is rated at, say, 12 volts, try and run it at 10 volts. Consider, also if practicable, feeding the lamps with a dc supply as opposed to the ac alternative; though they will operate on ac, using dc to power them will improve their longevity.

Always position filament lamps carefully and keep them well away from any plastic materials

Figure 67: 6.5-volt filament lamps wired in series, two lamps running from a 12-volt supply (above) and three lamps wired in series running from a 16-volt supply. Note in these illustrations that the lamps in both series connection groups are all the same voltage – 6.5 volts. There is no reason why mixed-voltage lamps cannot be used, eg on 16 volts a 12-volt and a 4-volt lamp could be series connected together across the supply so long as their total added voltage is equal to or just above the supply's voltage rating.

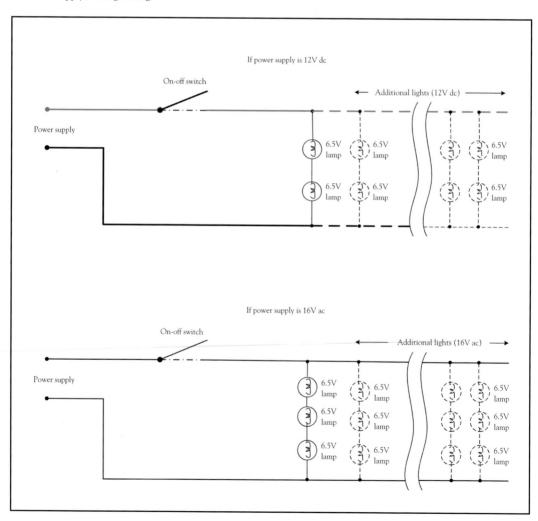

used in building construction as they will, due to their hot working temperature, cause the plastic to melt or distort.

Often the greatest drawback of these lamps is the current consumed by each one. Typically, GoW lamps will require some 60 to 80 milliamps each, so just 15 lamps will need between 900 milliamps (0.9A) and 1200 milliamps (1.2 amps). This is often easily overlooked by the newcomer where many lamps are connected to the PSU; the PSU's internal overload trip operates after a few moments and the modeller then wonders why all the lamps have gone out!

They do have one advantage in that if the lamp is rated below the PSU voltage you can, by series connecting them ('daisy chain' fashion), wire, for example, two 6-volt or three 5-volt lamps to run from a 12-volt supply. The only disadvantage here is that when one lamp fails all in that chain go out.

9
DIGITAL COMMAND CONTROL
(DCC)

The Digital Command Control system has taken the model railway world into the 21st century. It is such a leap forward that perhaps it can be compared with the change from clockwork to electric control of model trains. DCC allows multiple and totally independent locomotive operation all on one track-fed system. No isolating sections, individual track feeds or local control cabs are needed. One loco can remain stationary while a second is brought right up to it; they can even be coupled together. Double-heading is easily possible and even, if desired, full computer control.

Using the traditional dc system (what might be called an 'analogue' control system) to move a locomotive, we provide nominally between 0 and 12 volts dc to the rails. When full voltage is supplied the locomotive will move at the fastest speed the motor can muster. If we want the loco to run at half speed, the supplied voltage is

Figure 68: The simplest method of wiring a twin-looped layout for DCC operation (using insulated-frog points). Note the additional single wire connecting to one rail of the siding and to the same-handed rail on the loop. This ensures that the siding is always live regardless of the position of the point, and will then allow DCC locos into the siding, to have their lights or sound functions operating, or to allow them to be moved even with the point set for the main loop.

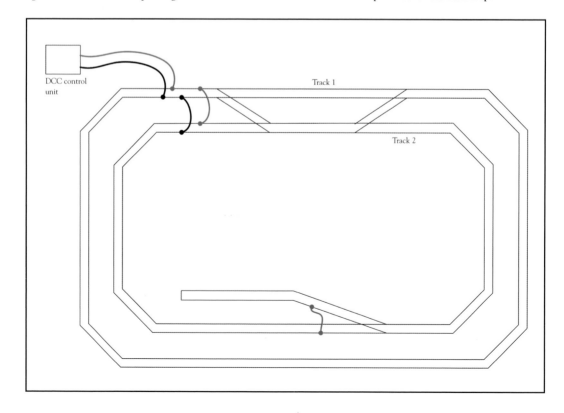

reduced by half (this isn't actually quite correct, but it is near enough for this example).

By contrast, the DCC system provides full voltage (around 16-18 volts in a sort of ac waveform) to the rails all the time and each loco has an 'on-board' DCC decoder fitted (microchips on very small circuit board). The decoder is connected to the rails via the loco's wheels. When a digital signal is sent out by the DCC controller or console it is received by the decoder, which then supplies the commanded voltage to the loco's motor – full volts for half the time will give half-speed running, or full volts for three-quarters of the time will give three-quarter speed, and so on. Technically this is called Pulse Width Modulation (PWM). Note that the decoder converts the ac input into dc for the motor power.

Every loco on the DCC-controlled rails is fitted with a decoder, and each loco's decoder is given a unique digital 'address' or number. All the loco's decoders receive all the data commands simultaneously, but only the decoder that has the unique digital address assigned to it will respond to that digital data signal being sent along the rails at that time; all the other locos' decoders will ignore the command. Once the decoder has seen the data arriving, it will act upon the commands and operate the device to which it is connected accordingly – motor,

lights, sounds, etc. Once it has been set, the device will remain at that setting until another unique command is received to turn off the function or alter the last setting.

Meanwhile the operator can call up the unique address number of another loco's decoder and a digital address can be sent to allow this loco to move off, while the first loco continues to run at its last setting. Hence we can now operate many locos simultaneously, and all on the same rails. For example, you could set the main-line train running, then call up a loco in a siding and carry out some shunting, etc, while the first loco continues to run uninterrupted. There is normally an 'All Stop' button provided on the controller for any emergency! This will stop everything and, once the problem has been resolved, you will need in most cases to restart each loco again in turn.

DCC not only allows you to control many locos at once, it also offers the opportunity to control signals, points, train lighting and sound effects. Add to this, in some systems, the option to have your computer running the railway and you can have a total and very realistic train control system. One advantage is that virtually all the DCC manufacturers' products are compatible and are produced to a set of defined standards written by the National Model Railroad Association (NMRA).

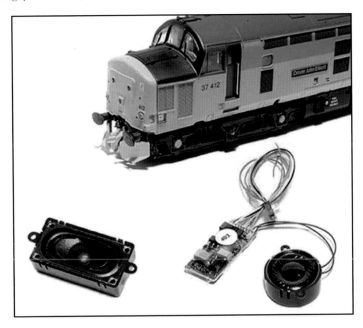

An ESU LokSound decoder and loudspeakers suitable for a Class 37 model, as supplied by South West Digital Ltd. *Photograph © and courtesy of Mr J. Humphreys*

DCC questions and answers

Q How do I fit a decoder?

A It all depends on the locomotive. Many modern locos are supplied as either 'DCC on board' (decoder factory-fitted) or 'DCC ready' (with a special socket into which a decoder can be plugged). Other locos need the decoder to be wired and soldered in, but in many cases this is quite simple, with only the split-chassis types needing more work.

Q Do I need to use Hornby decoders with Hornby locomotives?

A No. Generally you can pick and choose a suitable decoder from any manufacturer.

Q Do I need to use decoders from the same manufacturer as my command station?

A No. Almost all DCC equipment is made to a common defined set of standards, as set by the NMRA, so you can use whatever decoder is best suited to your locomotive or pocket. They should all operate with a different manufacturer's controller.

Q What about wiring for DCC?

A Don't be fooled by the 'just two wires' statement, although it's a lot simpler than you might expect, and usually much easier than conventional dc wiring. All you need to do is to provide power everywhere. There is no need to provide switched sections as with dc.

Q Can I run dc locomotives on my DCC layout?

A While some DCC systems allow this and it is technically possible, it is not recommended. This option works by 'stretching' half of the DCC signal to give a sort of dc bias. However, the loco is still running on what is basically an ac supply (hence the often high-pitched noise it makes when you put it on the track). The DCC track power can easily destroy the electric motor. Do this at your own risk and always remove stationary locos if they are to be left standing for more than a couple of minutes.

Q Can I run DCC locomotives on a dc layout?

A Yes. Most if not all decoders (check the decoder instructions) allow operation on a dc layout, though this can be disabled. The decoder detects the dc track power and responds accordingly. Do ensure that your dc layout doesn't have any electronic high-frequency track cleaners or feed-back controllers in use, as these can damage or confuse the decoder.

Q My DCC-ready loco moves OK, but the lights don't work with the decoder I have fitted, although they did work correctly on dc. What can I do?

A Try rotating the decoder plug through 180 degrees. It may have been fitted the wrong way around, which will give locomotive movement but no lights.

Q Can I mix DCC and dc controllers on the same layout?

A Not really. It is very likely to cause problems if the lines are connected. On two completely isolated or separate lines it is OK to do so, feeding one line with dc and the other with DCC. But if you connect together the tracks of a DCC and a dc layout, with no isolation between them, it will most likely damage your DCC controller or even both controllers!

Q Can I have two or more DCC consoles feeding the tracks at the same time?

A No. Never allow the outputs of two DCC consoles to become connected to the same rails, as serious damage can result. However, with certain systems you can have a second or third console ('slave') connected to the master console. This connection has to be carried out with a special linking cable running between the slave and master console. Special cables with equally special plugs and sockets are used to ensure that the correct connections are made, often using RJ12 connections.

Getting the best from DCC

Some basic DCC systems will state 'simple two-wire control', and while this is perhaps true, it isn't actually often the reality. All electrical power needs to get from its source to the motor, decoder or wherever it is needed as easily as possible. Electricity is basically lazy, and if an obstacle is placed in its path it won't try very hard to get over the problem – it just lays back and rolls over! This failure to reach its final destination is often due to a high-resistance joint. Imagine the power and data signals coming from the control console to the rails, from where they have to pass through numerous rail joiners (fishplates) to get from one track section to the next, and so on. Eventually the power arrives at the wheels of the loco, and has to reach the DCC decoder via, in most cases, wiper contacts touching the rear of the wheels. How many locations of possible high-resistance will the power have had to pass? Probably 40 or more! These include the clip connecting the power to the rails, two rail joiners per track section, point blades touching stock rails, loco wheels running on the rail surfaces, and the wiper contacts on the wheels taking the power to the decoder. Each of these is a possible high-resistance spot, and a possible cause for trouble! The main culprits are dirty rail surfaces, dirty wheels, dirty wheel wiper contacts and, of course, the loose or dirty rail joiners between the rails – quite a few obstacles, even without the possibility of the rail power clip itself being a poor connection.

How do you avoid these problems? Keep the rails clean with the aid of a track-cleaning rubber or special rail-cleaning fluid, and keep the loco's wheels clean with the aid of a wheel-cleaning brush set. Both the track rubber and the wheel-cleaning brush set are available from model shops from manufacturers such as Peco (also see Chapter 10). Cleaning the rails only needs to be undertaken once a week or so, as long as the layout is used regularly. However, if it is put away and not used for several weeks then the rails should be cleaned before every use, as they will most likely have tarnished. Keep the loco's wheels clean, and don't forget to clean all the rolling stock wheels too, as these also deposit dirt on the rails – improved running will result. (While these 'good practice' comments are aimed at the DCC user, some should also be observed by the dc user.)

For improved running, the DCC user can no longer rely on 'push-in' electrical connections such as track power connectors and rail joiners. If the track is not yet laid, solder the power wires (dropper wires) directly to the outside or the underneath of the rails. Also consider the improvement offered by running a DCC power 'bus' (two wires) around the underside of the layout and tap off this as many times as possible to feed sections of track. Nickel silver rail has a much greater resistance than copper wire, so the 'bus' offers improved supply voltages throughout the layout.

The DCC 'bus' will help to improve operations both electrically and data-wise. It is recommended that two DCC power wires (called the 'bus' from here on) are run around the railway in a radial circuit (see Figure 69). Connected to this bus are all the running rails and all accessories operated via DCC accessory decoders. Thus any problems such as high-resistance rail joiners will be overcome, as will volt-drop problems on larger layouts.

Ideally the DCC bus wire should be made from at least 1.5mm^2, or better still 2.5mm^2 solid wire – the wire used in domestic wiring cables is often ideal. A bus made with flexible wire is equally acceptable, but this needs to be of at least 32/0.2mm^2 or, for the larger layout, 50/0.2mm^2; flexible bus wire will be especially useful on portable layouts. There will be many connections between the bus and the running rails to ensure reliable data and power transfer to the rails and hence to the locos' wheels and decoders.

Having obtained the mains cable, carefully strip out the two insulated conductors from the outer sheathing. Discard the outer sheath and use the two insulated conductors (red/black or brown/blue). The bare earth wire can be saved and perhaps used as rail droppers or alternatively run round the layout and used as a common return bus for everything else that is not directly DCC-controlled.

Radial bus wires are perhaps the more normal method used for DCC bus wiring. 'Radial' means that the wires form a circuit, or start at one place,

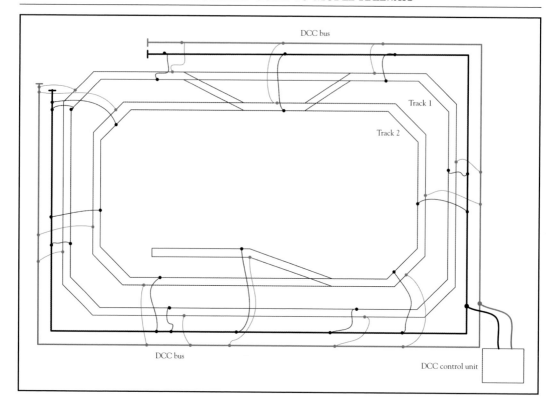

Figure 69: How the 'bus' is connected from the DCC control console unit via the two wires to the running rails. This is the same track layout as shown in Figure 68, where the feeds were only connected in two places. Using a bus and many dropper wires feeding the rails will improve electrical performance. Note that all the points shown here are the insulated-frog type.

normally the console, and terminate at the furthest point from it. A radial can also be wired as a 'T' configuration, where the console's output is taken in the same size of wire as is used for the main bus to a central or off-centre connection on the main bus wires, the 'top of the T' bus wires then run the length of the layout, terminating at each end. There is no reason why the bus should not be wired in a ring, where each bus wire starts and ends at the same place and is connected together to make a complete ring. Using a ring bus will effectually make the current-carrying and short-circuit path less likely to be effected by high-resistance wire run; however, its only advantage is where the layout is on one board and not an 'L' or 'U' shape, where a ring circuit would be very wasteful on bus wire.

Once the bus has been installed around the underside of the layout, connect the DCC base console unit's output terminals to the bus wires, using as short a length as possible of 24/0.2mm²

or 32/0.2mm² flexible wire, as 1.5mm² or 2.5mm² cable, or larger, will probably not fit into the console terminals. Then connect all the rails to the bus, ideally soldering all connections to ensure reliable data and current flow. Now we have a reliable bus (power and data highway) by which our locos can pick up power and data commands from the rails.

Having installed the DCC bus around the layout in a suitable-sized cable, it is now necessary to connect the bus to the rails. This is normally carried out using 16/0.2mm² flexible wires in the same two colours as the bus – red/black or brown/blue. This is called the 'dropper wire'. Solid copper wire droppers from the rails to below the baseboard could also be used, and the flexible dropper wire soldered to these; alternatively solder the dropper wire directly to the rail. See Chapter 6, which refers to this method of connection to the rail, which is the same as for a dc layout.

Above A typical DCC bus running around under the layout, wired in red and black insulated wire; the actual colour of the wire's insulation doesn't matter, so long as they are two different colours. The 16/02mm² droppers from the tracks above can be seen connecting with the bus wires. In the background can be seen a bare 1.5mm² copper wire, which is the common return wire for everything on the layout that is not DCC-operated, eg road and station platform lighting, colour light signals and point motors.

Right The use of a wagon to identify the 'red' rail, as described in the text.

Right A DCC bus and the many droppers running from the tracks above to connect with it, an arrangement that ensures quality operation and permanent feeds to all tracks.

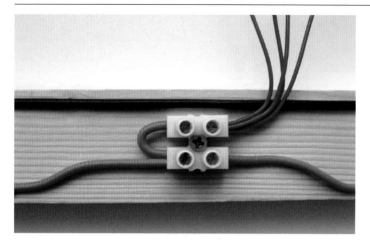

A 15-amp terminal block has been inserted into one side of the DCC bus wire and on the left a small link of the same bus wire connects from the lower 'through' terminal to the upper terminal. Connected to the right of this upper terminal are the dropper wires running off to the rails above. This method of bus connection is ideal for those who do not wish to make soldered connections under the baseboard. Always ensure that the grub screws are fully tightened down onto the stripped wire ends.

To help ensure that the correct dropper wires are connected to the correct rails, I have a very simple tip. Take a four-wheeled wagon and place a piece of tape – masking or electrical – along one side of the wagon. Place the wagon on one track with the taped side representing the rail immediately below it, which will become, say, the 'DCC red' connection. Now, without removing the wagon, run it around all the tracks by hand – use the points to pass from one line to another. Wherever the taped side on the wagon is, the rail directly under it is always connected to the red DCC supply – simple! Although I have said 'red', the choice of wiring colours is yours. But do only use two colours for all DCC track feeds and bus wiring, such as red and black or brown and blue, to ensure that the system of wiring is clear and easily understood.

All connections to the bus should ideally be soldered. Using a craft knife, simply remove a small portion of the bus cable insulation (about 20mm is ample) and wrap the track feed dropper wire around the bared wire. Apply a pre-tinned (wetted) hot soldering iron, wait a few seconds for the joint to heat, then apply a little cored solder to the joint – not the iron – until solder is seen to flow into the wires. Remove the iron and leave joint for at least 10 seconds to cool, then cut off any surplus dropper wire end. If you wish, a small amount of insulating tape can be wrapped around the joint to prevent it touching any other part of the bus or other circuit. Where a flexible wire bus has been installed, 'snap lock' clip-on connectors can be used; these automatically cut into the bus wire's insulation

and the dropper wire when closed up, and make contact between both. If you do not wish to solder or use 'snap lock' connectors, you could use 15-amp-rated screw terminal blocks cut up into one- or two-way pieces and used at the connection places.

Programming track

A 'programming track' output from the DCC console is available with most systems and requires a length of separate 'programme track' for setting up the 'address' and altering any 'configuration variable' (CV) settings (see below) of the on-board decoders in each loco. This track is powered from a special output on the base unit and, while not essential, it really helps in setting up a decoder. It also allows each loco's decoder to be programmed without causing any changes to the existing decoders already in locos on the main tracks. The programming track also normally provides a lower electrical current supply to the rails to prevent decoder burn-out should the decoder be installed incorrectly or should the loco be defective.

Consider for ease of use the end of one siding as this programming track, and wire this siding so that it has insulated rail joiners on both rails around 20 inches or so from the buffer stops. This section of track is then totally isolated from the rest of the line feeding into it. Now take two rail feeds connected to this length of track to either a Double Pole Double Throw centre-off toggle switch or a 3-way 4-pole rotary switch;

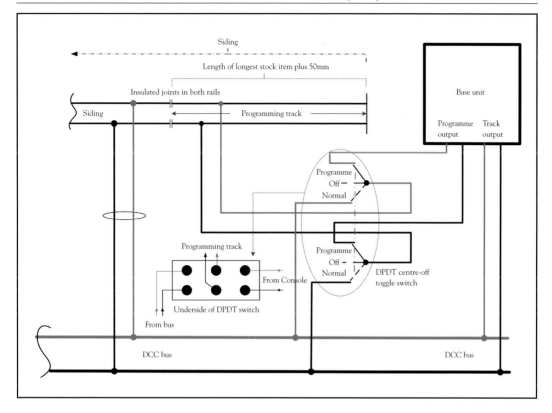

Figure 70: Wiring for a siding-end programming track with selectable switching

this will allow the siding track to be switched between 'Programme', 'Off' and 'Normal' running. If a rotary switch with four poles is used, an indication lamp (perhaps an LED) could be wired via one of the unused poles powered from an external non-DCC supply, to illuminate when the switch is in the 'Programme' function position. Figure 70 shows the set-up for a siding-end programming track with selectable switching.

If you do not wish to use the end of a siding for the programming track, you will need to use a totally separate length of track, laid and used solely for programming.

If your DCC console does not have a special 'programming track' output, an isolated section of track can still be used for programming and is wired as shown in Figure 71. When 'Programming' is selected on the switch, the feed to the main railway's rails or bus will be cut off, thereby preventing any accidental changing of addresses of locos that are still on the main tracks.

DCC operation with insulated-frog points

Insulated-frog points will require a small modification to enable full DCC operation. The simplest method is the addition of two link wires; alternatively, if a DCC bus is being used, run two new feeds from the bus to the two vee rails (see Figure 72). This conversion is all that is required to ensure that, no matter which way the point is set, DCC power is sent to all tracks, thereby keeping the entire track live regardless of which way the point is set.

One problem the DCC user may encounter with insulated-frog points is a sudden short-circuit occurring as a loco passes over the frog. These are sometimes caused by the metal wheels touching both rails where the rails are at their closest in both pre- and post-insulated frog area. This is more common on DCC-fed layouts as both rails are permanently powered with opposing polarities, and can cause the main control unit to detect the short-circuit and trip

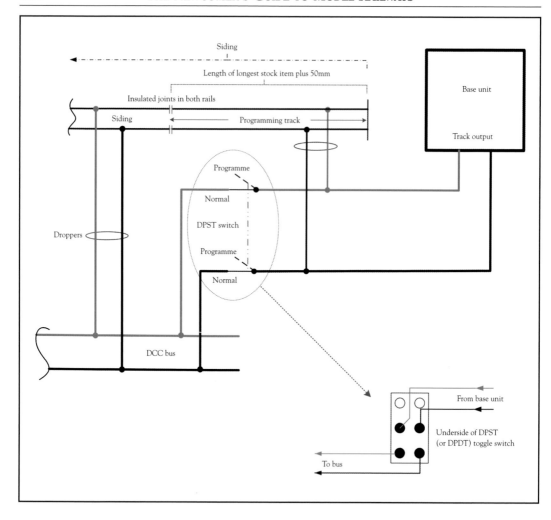

Above Figure 71: Wiring for an isolated section of track used for programming

Below Figure 72: Modification of insulated-frog points on a DCC layout by adding two linking wires

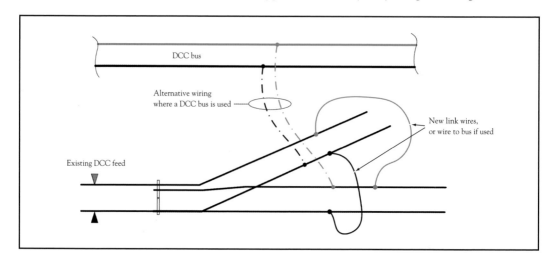

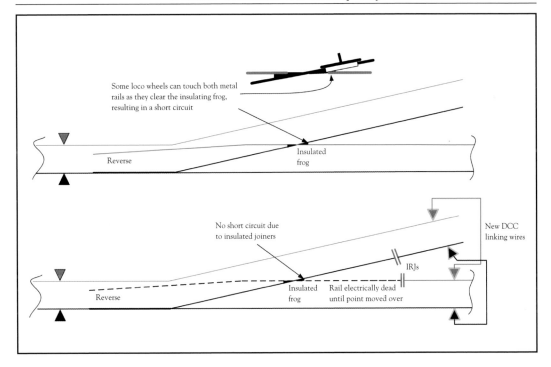

Figure 73: The upper drawing shows insulated-frog point track power switching and how short-circuits can occur on DCC layouts. The lower diagram shows how the problem can be eliminated by fitting two insulated rail joiners after the frog.

the internal overload device. The problem is easily overcome by fitting two insulated rail joiners after the frog at the ends of the two vee rails on any problematic point, then running in two linking wires from the two rails after the joiners and connecting them to the respective outer rails, as shown in Figure 73.

Decoder installation

Installation of a decoder in a loco will depend on several factors:

a) The age of the loco
b) The space available for the decoder's circuit board
c) Whether the loco is 'DCC ready', ie it has a decoder 6-, 8- or 21-pin NMRA DCC socket fitted inside by the manufacturer
d) Whether it has provision for a decoder

Only ever attempt to convert a loco to DCC that is proven to run well on conventional dc – converting a loco that runs badly on dc will result in equally or even worse running on a DCC system.

Stall current test

This test can be carried out on a non-DCC-fitted loco in order to discover the stall current drawn by the loco's motor, and determine the choice of decoder to be installed. To find out the stall current you will require a normal dc train controller, a length of track that is not connected to any part of the railway and a suitable dc-reading amp meter (a digital or analogue multimeter with a dc ampere range of at least 1.5 amps (for 'OO' locos). *Do not use the DCC-enabled track for this testing.*

Connect one wire from the conventional controller directly to one of the test-track rails, then connect the other controller's terminal to one side of a dc-reading amp meter. Connect the opposite terminal of the amp meter to the remaining rail. You now have a meter connected in series circuit! Place the loco on the test track and, holding it in place, turn up the controller to full power (see Figure 74). The meter should now be reading the normal motor running current flow.

Now stop the loco's wheels from turning – in other words, stall the motor. Note the current

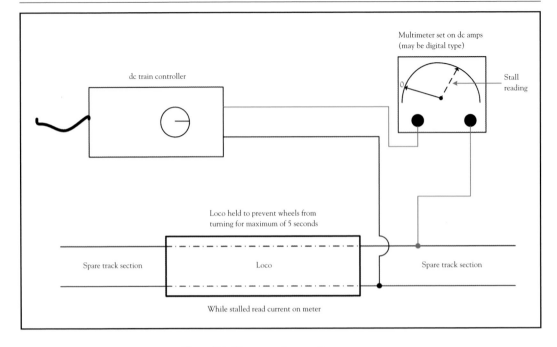

Figure 74: The set-up for a stall current test

being drawn on the meter. *Do not allow the stall condition to last for more than 5 seconds or the motor may burn out!* Once you have obtained the stall current reading, select a decoder that will handle the noted stall current. Most decoders will be rated between 1.0 and 2.0 amps dc continuous, though some are less! For 'OO' and 'N' gauge the use of a decoder rated at 0.5-1.0 amps is normally ideal. Larger gauges will require higher-output decoder currents and therefore a more specialist decoder.

Decoder configuration
The table below shows the configuration of an 8-pin three-function decoder. Note that the blue wire is common positive for all lighting functions.

Pin	Function	Wire colour
1	Motor right	Orange
2	Rear light(s)	Yellow
3	Function F1	Green
4	Left rail pick-up	Black
5	Motor left	Grey
6	Front light(s)	White
7	Function common	Blue
8	Right rail pick-up	Red

Compare this to an 8-pin single-function decoder. Note that pins 2 and 3 are not wired.

Pin	Function	Wire colour
1	Motor right	Orange
4	Left rail pick-up	Black
5	Motor left	Grey
6	Front light(s)	White
7	Function common	Blue
8	Right rail pick-up	Red

A four-function decoder will have a ninth wire, often purple, which is not connected to the 8-pin NEM plug. This wire, if not used, can be either cut off at the decoder's circuit board or have its free end insulated and tied back clear of all moving items; if it is required for a specific function within the loco, solder it to the appropriate function's negative lead and suitably insulate the joint.

'DCC ready' locos
When installing a decoder, first check whether the loco is 'DCC ready', which means that it is usually fitted with an NMRA decoder socket with a blanking plug, allowing conventional dc operation only.

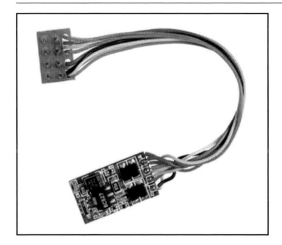

Above The NEM652 DCC 8-pin decoder plug.

Left A standard 8-pin DCC decoder.

If it thus fitted, carefully remove the body from the chassis; use the manufacture's servicing sheet for detailed information on which screws to remove or where to unclip the body to release it.

With the body removed, it is normal to see a factory-fitted printed circuit board, often located on top of the chassis and above the motor, although its actual position varies depending on the manufacturer. On this circuit board will normally be seen a small additional raised circuit board, which appears to have two or three solder blobs on its surface – this is the dc blanking plug. With the aid of a small screwdriver blade, carefully lift this blanking plug – it is a push fit into the socket below. Once the blanking plug has been removed, the 8-pin socket is visible. The No 1 pin position is often marked on the main circuit board by either a figure 1 or a small triangle mark.

Now insert the decoder's 8-pin plug into the socket, ensuring that the pin to which the orange wire is attached is at the No 1 position. If the plug is accidentally reversed no harm should come to either the decoder or the loco – all that will happen is that, when powered up, the loco will travel in the opposite direction from the console's setting, and if any lighting is fitted this may not work at all.

Once the plug is correctly and firmly in place, find a suitable place to locate the decoder. Place PVC insulating tape over any metal chassis areas where a decoder is to be sited, then use a double-sided adhesive pad to hold the decoder in place; if it is a steam loco, tuck it carefully inside the

boiler barrel, if space permits. Tidy up the wires from the decoder to the plug by using little pieces of insulating tape as necessary. Also ensure that no wires are likely to touch any moving parts.

Before refitting the body, place the loco on the programming track and check that it works correctly, then change its address from the default 03 to the one you have chosen (often the loco's running number or part of it). If all is working correctly, refit the body, ensuring that no wires or other items are trapped as it is replaced.

Note that locos in some scales will not have the 8-pin NEM socket fitted, but may have the 6-pin version. This is often found in 'N' gauge locos.

Non-'DCC ready' locos

If no decoder socket is present, it must be determined whether or not the motor and its brushes are in contact with any metal part of the chassis and hence to one or both of the rails via the wheels of the loco. To check if this is the case – and it is with a lot of non-DCC ready locos – once the motor's wiring has been carefully unsoldered and moved clear, its total isolation from the metal chassis can be determined by using a multimeter, switched to its ohms range, or a simple battery-operated buzzer. Check for a reading, or a buzz, between either side of the frame/chassis and both motor brush connections (or motor feed terminals if the brushes are not accessible). If a reading is obtained, the motor brushes or motor terminals must be fully insulated from the chassis. It is not possible to describe in detail how to achieve this, as every loco is of course different, but it is an essential process; it if it not undertaken the decoder will be totally ruined if power is applied to it and the motor is still in contact with one or both rails.

Once the motor is insulated, the existing wires from the wheels to the motor terminals need to be unsoldered at the motor end – make a note of which colour wire goes to which side of the loco. Once these two wires are removed, connect them to the red and black decoder wires by twisting and soldering the ends together. Note that, on steam-outline models, the red decoder wire connects to the right-hand side (looking forward) and the black to the left-hand side. Before soldering, cut a small length of heat-shrink tubing to cover the final joint and slide this onto one end of the wires, then twist and solder. Slip the heat-shrink tubing over the cooled soldered joint and gently warm the tubing until it has shrunk down and has made a nice insulated cover for the joint. Use the soldering iron's tip if you don't have a micro hot air tool. Now connect the orange wire to the motor terminal where the original right-hand wire was, then do the same with the grey wire, connecting it to where the left-hand wire was originally attached.

Other wires from the decoder are used to control lighting functions, such as head and tail lamps. Consult the decoder's manual for full information on these functions, although the two tables above list the common connections.

Several styles of motors are to be found in the 'OO' range, including 3- or 5-pole open frame, Ringfield and Can styles. Of all these, the Ringfield is probably the easiest to convert and is often found in older Hornby and Lima tender-drive steam locos and many Hornby and Lima diesel-outline locos and DMUs. 'N' gauge locos, especially steam-outline models, will require a physically smaller decoder due to the very limited space available inside the loco's body.

When converting an older loco, it is recommended that only the best-quality decoder is used, such as Lenz, TCS or Digitrax, to name but three of many currently available. This will ensure that the older-style motor performs at its very best.

The accompanying series of photographs describes the basic conversion technique for many 'generic' locos. I consider that split-chassis locos are probably the hardest to convert, but even these are not that hard – they just require a little more dismantling and plenty of testing during and after reassembly to ensure that there is no connection between the motor's terminals and either half of the chassis block.

The following sequence of photographs describes the conversion to DCC operation of this Hornby 'J94' 0-6-0 tank locomotive. It is not DCC ready, so it does not have an 8-pin factory-fitted socket inside and will therefore require the decoder to be hard-wired – all connections being soldered together.

Above Stage 1: Remove the body – referring to the manufacturer's service sheet – and also the metal weight that surrounds the motor. Keep all removed items secure on a small tray or in a box.

Below Stage 2: The motor has been removed from its housing and the wires running to the motor are ready to be unsoldered.

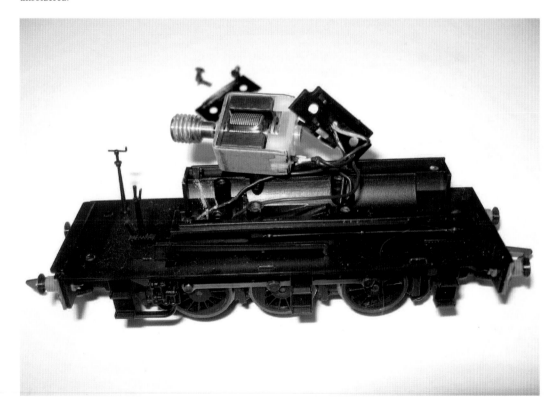

Above Stage 3: The motor is now completely removed and the original wiring is being made ready for the decoder wires to be connected to them.

Below Stage 4: The Bachmann decoder's red and black wires have been connected to the original wires from the wheels, and the joints are soldered. Two short lengths of heat-shrink tubing have been placed over the decoder's red and black wires ready to be slid over the soldered joints and shrunk down. The orange and grey wires will connect to the motor terminals.

Above Stage 5: The two orange and grey decoder wires are soldered onto the motor's terminals. Note the use of a short piece of small heat-shrink tubing to insulate the motor's upper tag and wire. In this loco the lower tag sits in an insulated plastic section, so there is no need to apply heat-shrink tubing to this tag.

Below Stage 6: The motor is refitted. The red and black decoder wires, previously soldered to the two wires removed from the motor that led up from the wheels, now have the heat-shrink tubing covering in place. The tubing is shrunk down to a tight fit over the joints by using a micro hot air blower or the heat of a soldering iron.

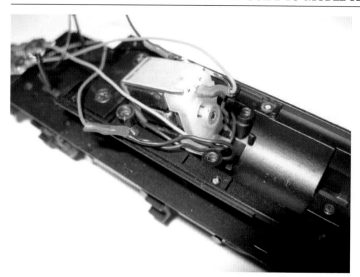

Left Stage 7: A closer view of the wire joints. Note that in this particular loco there are two original wires per wheel side that connect to each of the decoder's red and black wires. The joint between the red decoder wire and the two black wires can clearly be seen nearest the camera. The black decoder wire with its joint to the two other original wires is located behind the motor.

Above Stage 8: The metal weight has now been carefully refitted. The decoder in this locomotive is going to be housed inside the cab, as there was little room for it elsewhere inside the body shell. All the function wires (green, white, yellow and blue) have been carefully cut off at the decoder's circuit board as they are not required on this loco.

Below Stage 9: The decoder is in place and the body has been refitted. The loco will now be placed on the programming track and checked to ensure that it responds to the console, then its address will be altered from the factory pre-set 03 to,

in this case, '62' – the last two digits of the loco's running number. The Bachmann decoder is standing upright in the rear of the cab and is virtually invisible! Another option would be to remove the curved section of the ballast weight and locate the decoder in the hollow curved area that was used by the weight in front of the motor; however, this will reduce the loco's adhesion weight, and a small or micro decoder would be required to fit into the hollow.

Configuration variable (CV) settings

These control how the decoder operates the loco. Changing CVs can vastly improve the performance of a loco and also sets how the functions operate. CVs are normally adjusted while the loco is on the programming track (see above). Always take a note of which CV is being adjusted and from what value and by what amount, as later, if the loco does not perform correctly or not as expected, you can easily refer to the notes and convert back to the original settings or readjust to another CV value setting.

Configuration variable (CV) settings

CV No	M/O*	Description	CV No	M/O*	Description
1	M	Decoder address (default setting is normally 3)	25	O	Speed table
			26	O	Not currently used
2	O	Start voltage	27	O	Automatic stopping
3	O	Acceleration rate	28	O	Bi-directional
4	O	Deceleration rate			communication
5	O	Maximum (top) speed	29	M	Basic configuration register
6	O	Speed curve modifier			(direction and speed steps,
7	M	Manufacturer's version			etc)
		number8 M	30	O	Error information
		Manufacturer's ID number	31	O	Sub address
9	O	PWM period	32	O	Sub address flag
10	O	EMF feedback cut-out	33-46	O	Function outputs
11	O	Packet time-out	47-64	O	Manufacturer unique
12	O	Power source conversion	65	O	Kick start
13	O	Alternate mode function status F1 to F8	66	O	Forward trim
			67-94	O	Special speed table
14	O	Alternate mode function status F9 to F12	95	O	Reverse trim
			96-104	O	Not currently used
15	O	Decoder lock	105	O	User identifier 1
16	O	Decoder lock	106	O	User identifier 2
17	O	Extended address	107-111		Not currently used
18	O	Extended address	112-256	O	Manufacturer's use
19	O	Consist address	257-512		Not currently used
20	O	Not currently used	513-879		Not currently used
21	O	Consist address active for functions F1 to F8	880-891		Not currently used
			892	O	Decoder load
22	O	Consist address active for functions F9 to F12	893	O	Dynamic flag
			894	O	Coal/fuel
23	O	Acceleration adjustment	895	O	Water
24	O	Braking adjustment	896-1024	O	Sound and function modules

* Mandatory or Optional

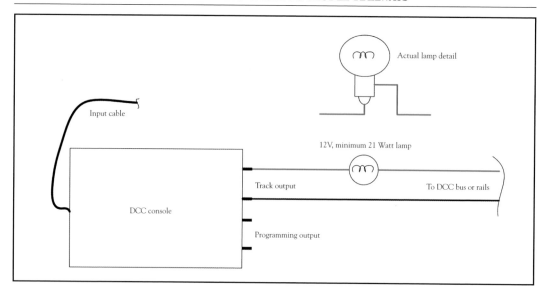

Above Figure 75: Using a car indicator lamp to warn of a short-circuit

Below Figure 76: The upper, simplified, diagram shows a conventional DCC bus with feeds to the rails, while the lower diagram shows the same layout with 'zonal' circuit-breakers and insulated rail joiners installed to form protected zones. Of course, in reality the zones would control a much larger area of track than shown here; for example, the whole station area could be one zone and the goods yard and sidings area another, so that a short-circuit in the goods yard would not effect the main lines.

The 12V, 21 Watt, lamp can also be used in place of the circuit breaker. Wire the lamp between the red bus wire and the rail, and wire the black bus wire directly to its rail. Should a short circuit occur in the lamp-protected zone the lamp will illuminate and leave the rest of the railway still working.

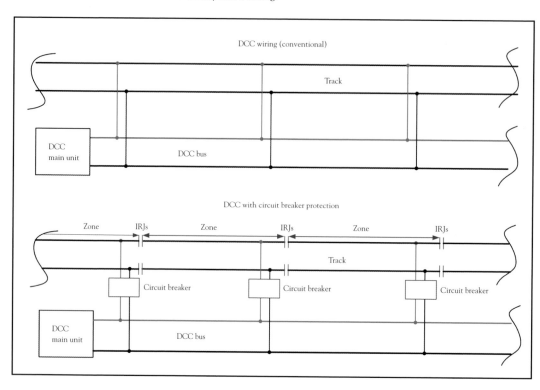

Over-current protection

There are several ways of preventing short-circuits from doing serious damage to the control system. The usual method is for the main DCC control unit to have its own built-in circuit-breaker, which in some units is fully self-resetting once the cause of the short-circuit has been removed. While this will provide overall protection, if it is tripped the whole layout stops, which is not always ideal!

Another method is to install a 12-volt 21-watt car indicator lamp in series with one feed wire between the console and the bus. The lamp will normally be extinguished, but in the event of a short-circuit it will illuminate and will usually prevent the main console's circuit-breaker from tripping (see Figure 75).

Also available are electronic 'zonal' short-circuit protection devices, into which the DCC bus is fed, then the output(s) are taken to the track via local buses (see Figure 76). These units are available in one, two or four individually operated zones on the same printed circuit board. These devices are very fast to operate and in most cases will trip long before the main DCC control unit has registered a current fault. They can also provide LED indication that they have operated, making fault-finding that much easier and faster.

Figure 77: A complete DCC power system of control, with track feeds, point and accessory feeds all derived from the main DCC bus. Note that power circuit-breakers are shown in all track feeds; although these are not absolutely necessary, they do offer improved fault protection and localise any short-circuit to just one section of track rather than shutting down the whole system.

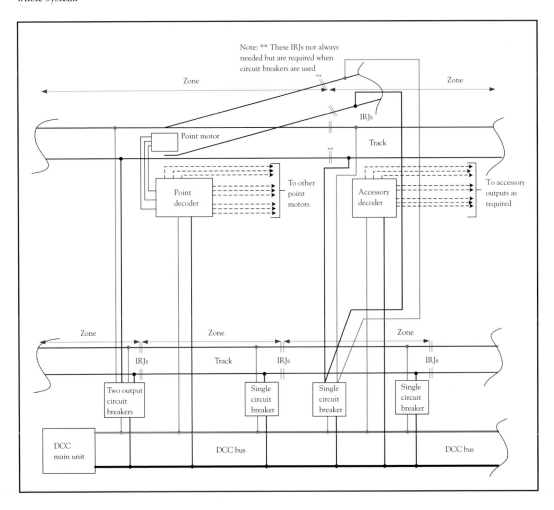

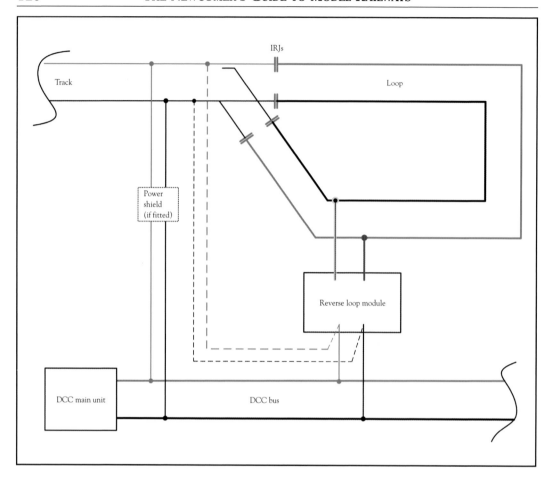

Figure 78: Wiring a reversing loop on a DCC-controlled layout

Reversing loops

Reversing loops on a DCC-operated layout require the fitting of a special reverse loop module. These modules often have four wires pre-attached by the manufacturer, or four terminals; two wires are attached to the DCC bus or the approach track rails and the other two directly to the rails of the loop. The loop must be totally insulated from the rest of the layout by the insertion of four insulated rail joiners at the entrance and exit (see Figure 78).

Turntables

On a conventional dc layout, the exit line of a turntable is normally the only powered track, when the table is aligned with that track. With DCC, locos can be stabled on any of the exit tracks with their lights or smoke units still functioning, or perhaps undertaking some minor shunting. However, some types of turntable can cause problems when a loco leaves or enters, as a short-circuit can occur due to the table rotating through 180 degrees and its rails becoming out of phase with the approach track.

In Figure 79 all tracks are live via the DCC bus (or from a connection onto the main approach track), while the rails on the table are fed via an automatic reverse loop module unit (this can be ignored if a split ring is used to feed the table rails). The exit or storage tracks for the turntable are often pre-wired to the turntable track by the manufacturer. If this is the case, insulate both rails on all approaching tracks just after the turntable and if necessary feed the rails on the table from a reverse loop module. The approach and all other storage

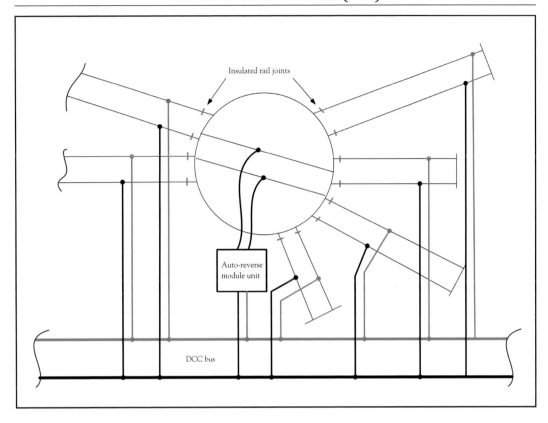

Above Figure 79: Wiring a turntable on a DCC-controlled layout

Below Figure 80: Powering lighting from the DCC bus. Note the 100µf electrolytic capacitor fitted across the output leads of the rectifier to give some smoothing to the circuit and, in the case of carriage lighting, a small amount of power when the carriages' wheels may not be fully in contact with both rails, for example when passing over insulated frogs. A simple on-off slide or toggle switch could be inserted into one of the DCC supply wires going to the rectifier as shown, to provide on-off selection.

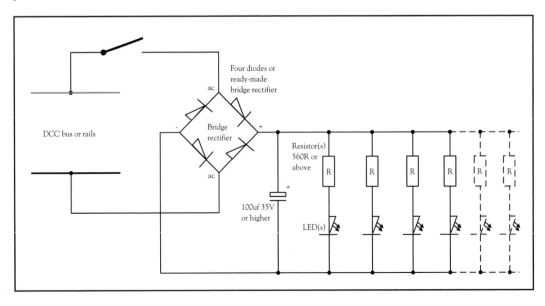

tracks are then wired directly to the DCC bus or the main approach track for their track power.

DCC lighting

DCC lighting can be powered directly from the DCC bus or rails, and can be used to illuminate LED carriage or building lights without the use of decoders. Some very basic electronic items can be obtained and soldered together to make a suitable circuit to connect directly onto the DCC bus or, in the case of carriage lighting, via a set of metal wheels on insulated axles and a pair of wheel wiping contacts. In Figure 80 the DCC power is being taken into a bridge rectifier. Either a ready-made bridge rectifier with a capacity of 1 to 3 amps can be used, or one can be made up by using four individual diodes, such as the 1N4002. From the dc output of the rectifier the power is then passed along to the individual LED(s) via their series resistors. The resistors need to be at least 560R or higher ohms and each LED has one resistor in its positive (Anode) leg. You can connect as few or as many LEDs as needed onto the outputs, as long as the maximum output of the rectifier is not exceeded.

10
MAINTENANCE AND TOOLS

There are several factors that can influence the running of the model railway. Excluding weather effects on an outdoor track, the following tips offer some advice on simple measures that can be taken to combat the main problems and improve everyday running.

Loco maintenance

If your layout, and especially the locos, have spent some years packed away in the loft or wherever, you will certainly need to strip down each loco and lubricate all the moving parts, as any original oil will have become a solid mass and no longer be able to lubricate as intended. I would not recommend trying to run any loco, no matter how great the temptation to do so, before carrying out basic maintenance, or it could lead to the motor itself burning out!

How to access the inside of a particular loco cannot be described here in detail as every one is different. Usually by studying the underside of the loco you can see how the manufacturer has assembled the chassis and bodywork. Some will have one, two or more small screws securing the two parts, while others will be a clip-fit and require gentle levering of the bodywork away from the chassis to free the two elements.

Where no manufacturer's service sheet is available, try, if possible, an internet search using the make and, if known, the model number of the loco; some manufacturers' websites have service sheets listed. Likewise, for much older models there may be websites run by enthusiasts or collectors, which may be able to offer advice or reprints of old service sheets.

The use of a servicing cradle is helpful to hold the loco upside down and prevent damage to any body details. Such a cradle, made in a U-shaped foam material, is available from Peco and suits most gauges up to 'OO'/'HO' scale.

Having determined how to gain access to the motor and gearing, you will generally be faced with three styles of electric motor: open frame, Ringfield or Can.

The open frame motor is the easiest to work on and service, and is often found in older pre-1980s locos. You can see the motors coils, the commutator and usually the motor brushes, which pass the current from the wheels to the motor coils.

The Ringfield type has a large 'pancake'-shaped electric motor with a series of gear cogs fitted to one side.

Finally, the Can type is now used by a number of leading manufactures and, most unfortunately, is often produced as a throw-away item and cannot be serviced! As its name suggests it looks like a small metal can with the motor shaft emerging from one end and perhaps either a much shorter length of shaft at the other end supported in the motor's end bearings or a longer shaft with a flywheel fitted; in some locos the shaft is extended to pass to another gear train, particularly in modern diesel or electric outline locomotives.

How does a dc electric motor work?
If you place an insulated coil of wire near a permanent magnet and apply a low-voltage dc current to the coil (typically 12 volts dc), the coil will be attracted to the magnet, or repelled if the current flow is reversed. Now take the coil of wire and wrap it around a circular former that can rotate freely and place the coil inside two permanent magnets of north and south magnetic poles. Apply dc power to the coil, and as it energises a magnetic pole is created within the coil's wire. Let us assume that it is positive when

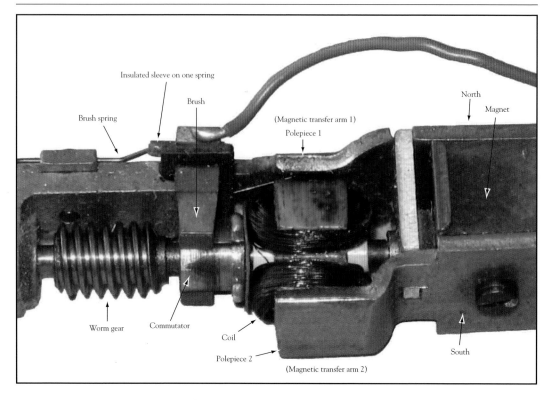

Insulated sleeve on one spring

Brush

Brush spring

North

Magnet

(Magnetic transfer arm 1)

Polepiece 1

Worm gear

Commutator

Coil

Polepiece 2

(Magnetic transfer arm 2)

South

Above **An old Tri-ang open frame motor showing the main components.**

Left **A typical Can-type motor, which is totally unserviceable by the user.**

it is opposite the permanent magnet's north pole – the coil is then giving a north. As the north pole produced by the magnet meets the north pole of the coil the magnetic forces repel each other ('like poles repel'). This magnetic force causes the coil to be pushed away (torque) and, as it is mounted on a rotating spindle, it starts to turn. As the turning movement continues, the coil's north comes under the influence of the opposite permanent magnet, which is giving a south pole; since dissimilar poles are attracted, the coil tries to pull towards the permanent south pole magnet. It is not able to do so fully and the pulling power of the magnetic field helps to give the rotating coil yet another pull

onwards. So now the rotating coil has moved through roughly half of its rotation and the current in it is now reversed. The coil is now fed with a positive supply via the other commutator segment and becomes a north pole; it is directly opposite the permanent north and the other side becomes a negative and south pole. Then, under the repelling north and south poles, it is forced around again and the cycle repeats.

In reality there are many turns of wire making each coil, and each coil is wound around a soft iron core to increase the magnetic field. Motors will generally have more than one coil – three, five or seven individual and electrically separate coils per motor is often the norm. Increasing the

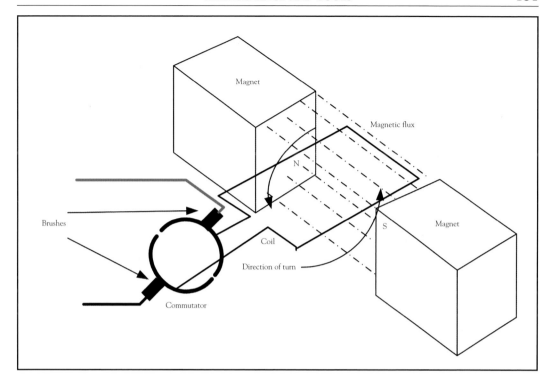

Figure 81: A very simplistic diagram showing how a dc motor works

voltage and current to the coils increases the magnetic strength, and subsequently the torque produced gives a faster rotation. Reversing the supply current reverses the rotational direction.

How are the coils fed and their polarity swapped every half cycle when it is spinning round? It is achieved by using a little device called a commutator. This is normally made from copper and is circular in format and divided up into segments that are insulated from each other. Pressing onto each side of the commutator are a pair of motor brushes, normally made from carbon and held in place by small springs. Direct current is fed into the carbon brush (picked up from the rails via the loco's wheels), passes into the commutator segment and then to the coil. It returns via the opposite-side commutator segment and the brush to the wheels and rails on the opposite side.

Thus our electric motor works on magnetism, both permanent and induced. One problem in the motors of older locos that often causes poor or slow running is the permanent magnet losing its magnetic strength; this is especially the case with old Hornby Dublo loco motors. The

magnet can be replaced or even remagnetised, which is a specialist job and requires a special machine. New replacement magnets are sold for some types of motor via specialist suppliers.

So, back to the maintenance. Once the loco's body has been removed, we can gain access to the motor and the gear drive train to the wheels. If you can see the commutator, now is the time to clean it and ensure that the brushes are in good order. Clean the commutator with a fibre pen to remove the build-up of old carbon deposits – do not use anything sharp that could scratch the commutator's surface. With the aid of a pin, carefully scrape along the line of the insulation that separates each segment. Carefully remove the carbon brushes and, if they are worn down, replace them; correct brushes are obtainable from good model shops or at times direct from the loco's manufacturer. The springs that hold the carbon brushes under tension must also be in good order and still provide the required tension.

Lubricate the two ends of the motor's shaft where it emerges from the motor casing and bearings.

Oil used for lubrication of model locos should only be of the light type; the use of special oil from model shops is ideal, and it often comes supplied in a tubular syringe-like applicator with a needle-like nozzle. The golden rule of model railway lubrication is that if you can see the oil on the part being lubricated, too much has probably been applied! A pin can be used, dipped in the oil then touched on the place to be lubricated to ensure that only the smallest amount of oil is applied.

Apply a little light grease to the worm gear and its mating cog, but again only use special grease, available from good model shops. Do not over-grease. Failure to use special model railway grease will lead to the grease warming up when the loco is running and becoming thinner, then, under centrifugal force, it will be thrown out and attach itself to the inside of your loco's body. Remember that, where a worm gear is used (most models with motors in the loco will use this method), you cannot turn the wheels to turn the motor as the worm gear train prevents this. Instead, gently turn the worm gear by finger

pressure and at the same time watch for the loco wheels to slowly revolve.

Lightly lubricate all the moving parts attached to the loco's wheels; this mainly applies to the valve gear and connecting rods on steam-outline models. Also check for any bent or binding rods or valve gear that may cause poor running. Carefully straighten any bent items; the use of tweezers or very fine long-nosed pliers is of help here.

Once all lubrication has been completed and the motor or worm gear turns the wheels freely, clean the wheels themselves, and check and adjust as necessary any wiping contacts that touch the wheels and transfer power to the motor. Use a fibre pen or an old small, blunt, flat-bladed screwdriver to scrape any 'muck' off *all* the wheels, not just the driving or pick-up wheels.

Now it is time to apply power to the loco. Do this by either placing the loco on the rails and applying a little power, or better still hold the loco upside-down and use a pair of short test leads with one end connected to the rails and the other end held onto the wheels that act as pick-

Servicing a modern diesel-outline 'OO' loco.

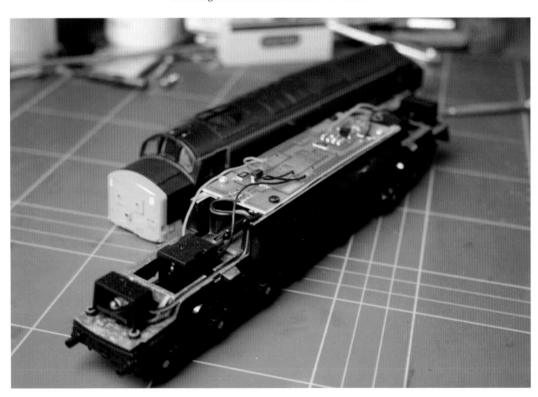

ups. Alternatively, use a Peco wheel-cleaning set, which passes track power via a wire brush and small scraper to the wheels, thereby both powering the loco and cleaning the powered wheels at the same time.

Assuming that the loco now runs as anticipated, give the motor a visual check under power. Look for excessive arcing between the brushes and motor commutator (don't worry if it's only a small amount, as there is always some); if it is excessive, turn off the power and rectify the problem. Often a lack of spring pressure on the brushes or the brushes not seating correctly on the commutator will be the cause, so a little tweak of the brush springs or the actual brushes will overcome the problem. Replace the brushes with new ones if they are excessively worn. If the arcing cannot be reduced, it is possible that one of the motor coils has burned out and is shorting internally. Unfortunately in this case there is very little that can be done other than replace the motor. Some motors can be rewound by a specialist, but this is an expensive option and is only used on valuable models that cannot be repaired in any other way.

Any smoking in the motor or failure to rotate under power – perhaps producing just a buzzing noise – must be dealt with straight away. In both cases, turn off the power immediately. Smoking is normally a sign that the motor's coils are short-circuiting, while a failure to rotate can be from the same cause, a very stiff final drive mechanism or seized motor bearings. Further detailed examination will be required, and motor replacement may be necessary.

Many people report that their Ringfield motors always squeal when they are run for a few minutes. This is mainly due to lack of lubrication; applying a drop of the previously mentioned light oil to both sides of the motor bearings, where its spindle emerges from the motor casing, will often resolve the problem.

In reality, there is little the ordinary modeller can actually repair on many models today. Failed parts are now normally completely replaced with a new item. However, general maintenance servicing should still be undertaken frequently by carrying out light lubrication and greasing of moving parts, not forgetting the cleaning of all the wheels and any wiping wheel contacts.

Track maintenance

Track maintenance also needs to be undertaken on a regular basis. The keeping of the rail tops and, wherever possible, their inner top edges spotlessly clean is the means to ensuring that your layout operates faultlessly electrically – this is especially true with a DCC layout. Rail-cleaning is on a par with wheel-cleaning!

Never use anything that is abrasive to clean the rails' surface as this will cause minute scratches that in turn will lead to increased dirt contamination and increased cleaning – a vicious circle!

A proprietary rail-cleaning block or track rubber such as those sold by Peco or Hornby will remove most surface dirt, especially if the layout has not been used for some while. Once the rails are cleaned they can be kept in this condition without quite so much hard work by using a liquid rail cleaner, though the use of the track rubber is still needed occasionally. I use Isopropyl Alcohol (IPA), which is perhaps a little on the expensive side, but it leaves no residue once it has been applied as it simply evaporates. The IPA can be applied by hand with the aid of a lint-free cotton cloth – an old handkerchief is ideal – or by using one of the specially produced track-cleaning tanker wagons. The IPA is poured into the wagon, which has special cleaning pads fitted underneath that spread the fluid onto the

A typical track cleaning rubber. *Courtesy of and © copyright Hornby Hobbies Ltd*

rails and also help to wipe the surface clean. The tanker wagon is towed or pushed around the layout with the aid of a loco, cleaning as it goes.

Electrical conductivity via the metal rail joiners is something often overlooked by the newcomer, but it is essential that the joiners are maintained and are kept clean and tight, especially if they are the primary means of transferring track power from one rail to the next. If the track sections are taken apart and reassembled regularly, or if you are relaying some track that hasn't been used for a while, before fitting the rails together clean the rail ends where the joiners will fit and also the insides of the rail joiners, ideally using a fibre pen; the pen's fibre bristles will easily slip inside the open area of the rail joiners and 'scrub clean' the inside surfaces.

Additionally, once a rail joiner has been correctly fitted onto a rail end, use a pair of long-nosed pliers to carefully squeeze up the sides of the joiner onto the lower sides of the rail. This will help improve the electrical connection between tracks. Do not forget that the 'squeeze' should be carried out at both ends of each joiner.

On points, use a fibre pen to clean the inside edges of the stock rails where the switch rail touches it. Similarly brush clean the inside faces of the moving switch rail.

Tools

Modellers need to acquire a selection of tools to enable themselves to undertake the various tasks required. The tool kit does not necessarily have to be vast, but some easily obtainable tools are the 'bread and butter' of modelling, while some will need to be a specialist purchase.

Basic tools

The basic tool kit should ideally contain some if not all of the following items, listed in alphabetical order:

Adhesives – including woodworking PVA, 'superglue', impact adhesive and UHU-type general glue
Craft knife – both small and heavy duty (eg Stanley knife) types
Electric drill – mains or cordless battery-powered
Hand wheel brace (drill)
HSS drill bits – selection from 1.0mm to 6.5mm
Micro screwdriver set – often with five or six crosshead and flat blade drivers in a flip-top box (sometimes referred to as jeweller's or instrument screwdrivers)
Mitre block

Mitre block

Various types of pliers and wire cutters

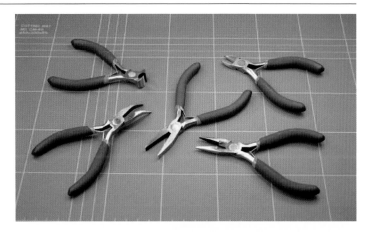

All photographs © and reproduced with the kind permission of Expo Drills and Tools

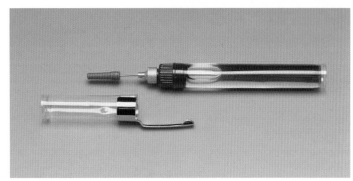

Precision oiler or lubricator

Panel saw
Pencil
Plastic clamps – small and medium openings (often sold in packs of four)
Pliers and wire cutters – various types
Precision oiler or lubricator
Screwdrivers – crosshead and flat blade types
Set square
Soldering iron – 18 to 25 watt with stand
Steel rule – 12 inches (300mm)
Steel tape measure – 3-metre type
Tack hammer – 4 ounce

Specialist tools

Specialist tools include, but are not restricted to, the following:

1.5lb (24oz or 0.72kg) ball pein hammer
Adjustable combination set square – 12 inches (300mm)
Archimedes drill
Automatic wire strippers
Back-to-back gauge – to suit your chosen gauge
Bench vice
Coping saw

Archimedes drill

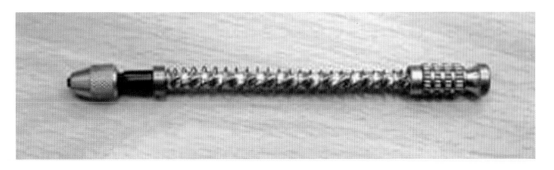

Digital multimeter

All photographs © and reproduced with the kind permission of Expo Drills and Tools

Fibre pen

Digital multimeter – capable of reading dc amps, ohms, and ac and dc volts
Electric jigsaw
Electric mitre saw (chop saw)
Electrically powered small lathe
Fibre pen
File – smooth-cut, 10-12 inches
Files – needle-type in assorted shapes
G clamps – various widths
Gas-powered soldering iron kit
HSS drill set – selection from 6mm to 10mm
Magnifying workbench lamp
Micro drill set – 0.1mm to 1.5mm
Mini electric drill – eg Dremel.

Panel pin punch
Razor saw
Safety cutting rule
Scalpel-style knife – and supply of replacement blades
Scriber
Self-healing cutting mat
Solder sucker tool
Tap and die sets – metric sizes from M0.5 and BA sizes 12BA.
Taper broaches
Tapered reamer to 10mm
Thermostatically controlled soldering iron station

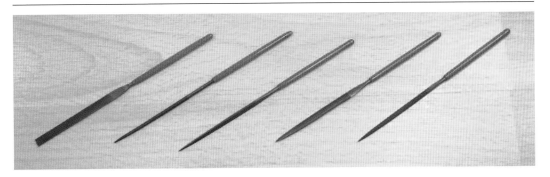

Above Assortment of needle files

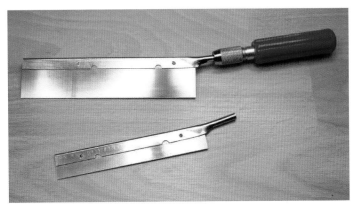

Right Razor saw

Tool box – cantilever or lift-out-tray type
Track rail gauge – to suit your chosen gauge
Tweezers – both normally open and closed types
Woodworking hand mitre saw – approximately
    600mm blade
Woodworking countersunk bit
Work bench – for general light-duty work.
'Workmate'-style workbench

While these lists may seem daunting, the tools will not all need to be purchased in one go. Buying a quality tool every month or so will slowly allow you to build up a good selection.

Whenever possible only purchase quality tools such as those manufactured for trade use; treated with respect, they will last a lifetime.

Solder sucker tool

GLOSSARY

Abutment A supporting structure on either side of a bridge or arch

Accessory An item that is not part of the train or its rolling stock, eg station, platform, points and signals, etc

Accessory decoder A DCC decoder used to operate accessories such as points and signals

Address The unique number allocated to a locomotive's DCC decoder or accessory decoder

Adhesion The contact between two surfaces, typically wheels to rail

Alternating current (ac) A current that changes polarity (or frequency) and current flow at preset intervals; UK mains ac is at 50Hz

Ampere (amp) A measure of electric current flow

Analogue In model railways, a standard (nominal) 12-volt dc control system

Anode The positive end or connection of an electronic device, denoted by the letter A

Ballast The small stones that retain the track in position

Baseboard The structure on which the model railway is supported

Bogie Small-wheeled centrally pivoted truck attached to and supporting the underframe of a locomotive

Boiler The steam-producing area of a steam locomotive

Booster A DCC device for increasing the power available to the rails

Brush (motor) A device used to transfer electrical power to the motor commutator

Bus A wire or solid bar that provides a continuous path to the flow of electricity, and to which are connected various wires to feed equipment

Cab 1) The enclosure on a locomotive from which the driver operates it
2) The device that the model railway operator uses to control the speed and direction of a locomotive

Cab control A means of controlling one or more trains within a specified section of the model railway

Capacitor Discharge Unit (CDU) A device installed into the wiring of solenoid point motors immediately after the PSU and before the point lever switches, to give a pulse of higher power to the solenoid coils, ensuring reliable movement, especially where two or more coils are operated at once from a single switch

Cathode The negative end or connection of an electronic device, denoted by the letter K

Chipboard A board manufactured from particles (chips) of wood bonded together with a resin adhesive

Coil An electrical winding providing a means of converting electrical power into mechanical movement, as used to power a loco motor or point motor.

Command station The electronic control centre of a DCC system (see also Console)

Common return A means of returning all electrical feeds to their appropriate transformer connections over just one wire

Commutator The circular segments on an electric motor that transfer power to the motor coils

Configuration variable (CV) Adjustable parameters on a DCC decoder, whereby the user can alter the settings preset by the decoder manufacturer, enabling speed, direction, acceleration, deceleration rates, etc, to be adjusted and fine-tuned

Consist Under DCC control, the means of coupling two or more locomotives together and giving the whole group one address number and controlling all locos within that group (or consist) from one setting; in the UK this is known as 'double heading'.

Console The master control position or the electronic processing unit in a DCC system

Controller The means by which the locomotive's or train's speed is set

Crossing The place where one track meets another in a point or 'diamond' track configuration

Crossover A configuration of two sets of points enabling moves to be made between parallel tracks

Current The amount of flow of electricity in the circuit (see also Ampere)

Cut-out A circuit-breaker

Cutting That part of a railway where it passes through a hillside, which has been partially removed to allow the railway to continue at one level

Decoder A small printed circuit board fitted with electronic components, which controls a DCC locomotive's motor, lights and sounds or accessories

Diagram A means of representing what is being provided on the model, for example wiring or track plans, drawn to show their relationship to the real thing

Diesel A compression-ignition engine, or a type of locomotive using a diesel engine to power it

Digital Command Control (DCC) A system used to control many locomotives and accessories at once by means of a digital signal flowing along the rails
'DCC fitted' (also known as 'DCC on board') means a loco that has a factory-fitted DCC decoder installed. Most can also be run on conventional dc-powered tracks
'DCC ready' means a dc locomotive that has a factory-fitted decoder socket installed, but can only be operated on dc layouts until the dc plug is removed and a suitable decoder is fitted in its place, when the loco becomes DCC-operable

Direct current (dc) An electric current that flows in one direction only

Distant signal A signal that advises the train driver of the position of Stop signals in the section of track ahead; when the Distant is 'on' (yellow), it indicates that the next Stop signal is also 'on' (Danger, or red)

Dropper A track feed wire connected to the running rail's side or underside and passed down through the baseboard to make further contact with other wiring

Earth (electrical) An electrical connection to the ground, used as a safety measure

'Electrofrog' The frog area of a point that is constructed from all-metal rails

Embankment The raising up above the surrounding ground of the railway to maintain its level

Engine In model railway terms, a locomotive

Fiddle yard An 'off-stage' area, often at the end of a layout, perhaps consisting of a series of fanned sidings where the rolling stock is held and reassembled ready to reappear as necessary

Filament lamp A tungsten lamp normally comprising of a wire-wound filament contained within a sealed glass envelope

Fishplate The metal plate joining together two abutting lengths of rail

Flange The projecting rim or edge of a wheel that guides it in the required direction and keeps it on the rails

Frog The crossing place of the two rails leading away from a point's switch rails

Function A DCC decoder-enabled switch, used to operate lights, sounds or other accessories

Gauge The distance between the inside faces of the two running rails

'Grain of rice' (GoR) A micro-miniature filament lamp normally operating in the range of 1.5 to 16 volts, and supplied fitted with wire leads

'Grain of wheat' (GoW) A lamp similar to, but slightly larger than, a GoR lamp

Hertz (Hz) 1 hertz is 1 cycle per second (typically, what is being counted is a complete cycle); thus 100Hz means 100 cycles per second, and so on. UK ac mains is at 50Hz

'Insulfrog' The insulated frog area of a point or crossing

Level crossing A place where the road crosses

the railway on the level; it may be open, gated or protected by barriers

Lever A device to operate an item that is often remote from the actual place of operation, eg a signal box lever or a model point lever

Light Emitting Diode (LED) A device that, when fed with low-voltage dc in one direction, emits light

Locomotive The engine that pulls or pushes a train of coaches or wagons

Locomotive address A DCC term – see Address

Loop A continuous circular connection

Medium Density Fibreboard (MDF) A smooth-surfaced wood-like board used for baseboards or side framing

Mimic panel A panel or console that carries a miniature version of the layout's track plan on its surface, as well as switches for point and signal control, and track isolation switches on dc-powered layouts. It may also have a dc layout's train controllers mounted in it

Motor An electrical device for powering a train or moving a point

Multiple Aspect Signalling (MAS) A system of colour light signalling that can display more than one colour aspect, usually red, yellow, green or double yellow

Narrow gauge A term applied to any railway whose gauge is less than the 'standard gauge' of 4ft 8½in

National Model Railroad Association of America (NMRA) A body that controls the standards of railway modelling in the USA and sets the standards for DCC worldwide

Normal The position of a point when set for the normally straight-ahead movement (but could also refer to a diverging line if that is the main route)

Off 1) The position of a signal when it is cleared to allow a train to proceed
2) The position of a switch when the contacts are open and preventing the flow of electricity

On 1) The position of a signal when it is at Stop or Caution
2) The position of a switch when the contacts are making and allowing the flow of electricity

Permanent way The trackbed and track in their finally laid position

Pick-up An electrical connection, normally between a loco's wheels and the wire to the motor

Platelayer A track maintenance person

Plywood A lamination of three or five thin sheets to produce a strong, easily cut sheet material

Points The means by which trains can move between different tracks

Polarity A voltage that can be positive or negative with respect to some other voltage, as at the other end of a battery or electric circuit

Power Supply Unit (PSU) A normally mains-powered and often totally encased unit containing one or more transformers supplying the safe low volts required for a model railway

Programming A DCC term for setting the 'configuration variable' (CV) settings of a decoder

Programming on the Main (PoM) A DCC term for the ability to set configuration variables while the loco is on the main layout track

Programming track A DCC term for a special length of track that is isolated from the main layout and where decoder CV values are adjusted

Propelling A reversing move by a locomotive whereby it is pushing rather than pulling a train

PSE Planed Square Edge timber

PSU See Power Supply Unit

PVA Polyvinyl acetate, normally a water-based polymer adhesive that is ideal for bonding wood to wood or paper and cardboard to one another in model building construction, bonding scatter materials to the sub-base surface, and, diluted with water, for bonding real stone ballast It normally dries clear or translucent

Radial A circuit or wire that does not return back to its source

Rectifier A device that converts ac current into dc current

Relay An electrical switch that opens and closes its contacts under the control of another electrical circuit

Reverse The position of a point when set for movements away from the straight ahead or normal main-line route

Reverse Loop Module A DCC device that automatically swaps over the output supply upon detecting a short-circuit at the input, thereby removing the short-circuit

Reversing Allowing the direction of travel to be changed to go backwards

Ring A circuit that starts and ends at the same source

Rolling stock Any item of rail-mounted vehicle that is not normally powered, such as coaches and wagons

Route The direction a train is to take

Scale The ratio of the relationship between the real thing and the model

Scratch building The construction of a building or item of rolling stock from a basic selection of sheet materials as opposed to the use of a kit

Semaphore A type of signal with a mechanically operated pivoting arm that can be raised ('upper quadrant') or lowered ('lower quadrant') approximately 45 degrees from the horizontal to give a 'proceed' aspect. Semaphore Stop signals indicate Danger when in the horizontal position, while Distant signals, when horizontal, indicate 'proceed with caution', as the next Stop signal will be at Danger.

Siding A subsidiary line connected to the main line used to stable or accommodate trains or locomotives

Signal A lineside device used to control the movement of trains

Signal box A building housing the equipment for the operation of points and signals over a particular section of track

Sleeper A wooden, steel or concrete beam that holds the rails apart to the correct gauge

Soldering The joining together of two or more wires or pieces of metal by melting a low-temperature metal (solder) into the joint and allowing it to cool and set

Solenoid An electrically powered coil that, when energised, will attract metal by induced magnetism

Switch A device for turn on or off, or divert, the flow of electricity

Terminal 1) The end or departure point of a railway line, usually with station buildings and platforms
2) An electrical connection where the ends of two or more wires are joined together

Transformer An electrical device that converts by magnetic induction an ac input voltage to another ac voltage. The output can be higher ('step up') or lower ('step down') than, or the same ('1 to 1') as the input volts. In the case of model railway transformers, normally the output is totally separate electrically from the input, eg an isolating transformer of the 'step down' type

Weathering The art of making a model look as though it has been aged or used out of doors

Wiring The run of one or more wires making up the layout's electrical control paths

BIBLIOGRAPHY

Recommended reading and sources of further information are as follows:

Amos, Roger *The Complete Book of Model Railway Electronics*
Freezer, C. J. *The PSL Book of Model Railway Track Plans*
 The PSL Book of Model Railway Wiring
Morton, Ian *Aspects of Modelling: Digital Command Control*
Peco/*Railway Modeller*, 'Shows You How' series of booklets

Monthly (UK) magazines:
British Railway Modelling
Continental Modeller
Hornby Magazine
Model Rail
Model Railway Journal
Railway Modeller

Suggested websites:
www.brian-lambert.co.uk
www.metcalfemodels.com
www.modelrailforum.com
www.mremag.com
www.mrt.org.uk
www.newrailwaymodellers.co.uk
www.rmweb.co.uk
www.scalescenes.com
www.superquick.co.uk

The end ... or perhaps just the beginning?

INDEX